INTO THE WIND

JOURNEY OF AN ENTREPRENEUR

WILLIAM P. BUTLER

CHAMP REALTY INVESTMENT CORPORATION | COVINGTON, KENTUCKY

Published by
Champ Realty Investment Corporation | Covington, Kentucky

Publisher's Cataloging-in-Publication Data
Butler, William P.

Into the wind : journey of an entrepreneur / William P. Butler. –
Covington, KY : Champ Realty Investment Corporation, 2023.

p. ; cm.

ISBN13: 978-0-9601209-0-1

1. Butler, William P. 2. Businessmen--United States--Biography.
3. Success in business. I. Title.

HC102.5.B87 A3 2023
338.092--dc23

Project coordination by Jenkins Group, Inc. | www.jenkinsgroupinc.com

Interior design by Brooke Camfield

Printed in the United States of America
27 26 25 24 23 • 5 4 3 2 1

Dedication

To Sue, my wife and life partner on the journey. You have supported me and shared with me fully in both worldly and spiritual growth. You have guided and reined me. You have gifted me with your unending love and commitment.

About the Cover

I have always had an affinity with the eagle. I have collected large, hand-carved eagle sculptures. Those that I purchase must be a nearly perfect likeness to the actual bird.

The eagle flies higher than nearly any other creature of the sky, is the symbol of strength, courage, our country's standard for freedom, liberty, and independence. The eagle has eyesight 10 times greater than humans and can spot its prey from afar. The eagle is a survivor and has existed in its present form since before the time of Christ. And yet, for all its grandeur, is a scavenger—for me a sign of humility!

Contents

Part III:
Builder of People

Part IV:
Building Communities

Two roads diverged in a wood, and I—
I took the one less traveled by,
And that has made all the difference.

—Robert Frost

Preface

For years, when people heard the stories of my experiences guiding Corporex through major economic recessions, or about the projects and the many other events of the past 57 years in business, they would say, "You have to write a book!" My quick response was always, "Who will read it?"

When I was in my teens, the period I call the idealistic years, I wrote poetry. One line I wrote back then stuck with me forever: "It is not for me to catalogue the man." I'm not sure I was even a man yet when I wrote it, but I know I was looking into the future at the time, thinking about who I wanted to be and my purpose. I do not know why that statement was important to me, or why it prevailed in my mind vividly for all these years; but that sentiment did initially keep me from undertaking this task.

I do so with the intention that this will not be an autobiography. There had to be an overarching purpose of a higher order to justify tackling the challenge of penning a book-length work. While it is impossible to separate the career from the man, my commitment is to share stories, experiences that are both interesting and hopefully helpful to the reader. Foremost in my mind as I write are, of course, my children and their children, and maybe their children; the great and loyal employees who have helped the company to achieve what has been accomplished, and maybe their families too will recognize their mom and dad's contribution and be proud; and then all the myriad people who have supported us along the way, including our board members, as well as the bankers, contractors, and vendors—and some special friends whom I have been blessed to know and with whom I have shared significant parts of my life. I sincerely hope the narrative that follows lives up to my intention in undertaking this task.

Writing a book is a fascinating experience. For one, it is somewhat therapeutic. The process requires that one go back, repeatedly, to be reminded of events and meaningful outcomes that were frankly forgotten, to see more than 70 years of life from the very beginning. Those very early years speak loudly about what how and why I became who I am. It is like coming full circle.

I thought I had discovered everything there is to know about myself and my life's special experiences, like my spiritual encounters. Not so. The process of reflection and retelling brings forth many more discoveries by looking back and seeing the entire experience as a whole.

For example, I came to realize how appreciative I am of my parents—two people who gave me this incredible opportunity. Without them, in particular, I would not have been inducted into the value system I cherish. Their introduction to the religious way in life at an early age led me ultimately to a higher spirituality. Without them, I may not have come to know God, the One I call the Source, the Light, and certainly not with the understanding I feel has been my reward for openness. I may not have come to comprehend that the Source of the energy of the universe, and simultaneously that energy which fuels each of us every day, is the same energy we know as a four-letter word: L-O-V-E. These are but a few of the fruits of this life which they gave me and which I am even more grateful for today.

I have had the privilege of following my ideas, trying to turn them into reality—always with a purpose. Sometimes I wonder where my creativity, or what others have called visionary skills, originated. Is it human, or is it more than that? Is it an extension of the love energy? Why me? I suppose above all else, this is my gift, and I hope I have used it and directed it for the good at all times. If one accepts, as is often stated in searching spiritual conversations, "that all things happen for a reason," the concept that we lived life before, that our soul is continuous even when without a body, then this life may not be the last. To such awareness my visionary dimension has made me receptive and has opened many doors indeed, not only in a spiritual way, but in my work, in investments, in contributions, in every walk of this career journey.

My hope is that this book not only tells the story of Corporex, of the Northern Kentucky community, and of my God experiences but also addresses purpose and service and contribution through the lens of my own blessed life history, with a look ahead to what I know are the future possibilities for each of us who share the work and the life of our time.

William P. Butler
Covington, Kentucky
March 2023

Part I

The Formative Years

"When you are age 18,
you are on your own."

–MOM

Chapter 1

Where the Journey Begins

Anyone who has ever driven the John A. Roebling Suspension Bridge from Cincinnati, Ohio, into Covington, Kentucky, will likely understand the dynamic that exists between the metropolitan community to the north and Northern Kentucky, the home of Corporex Companies, LLC, to the south. Cincinnati, long ago referred to as "the Paris of America," and thereafter as the Queen City, sits only 14 feet higher above sea level than the Kentucky shore of the Ohio River, but that has made all the difference in the evolution of these respective communities over the past 200 years.

Fourteen feet may not seem like a lot, but when considered in the context of the period, when pioneers navigated the rivers in their travels westward back in the 1500s and 1600s, this was critical. They actually first chose the Kentucky shores of what became Covington and Newport because they were easier to access from the water—land that was in a flat river basin with lots of topsoil for farming. But it also flooded regularly and predictably. This problem was not solved until after World War II by building flood barriers. That simple discovery about why the Northern Kentucky community where I was born and raised did not develop like Cincinnati was what caused me to develop the most high-risk property of my career—the Towers of Rivercenter—in a location where no such investments had been made in over 100 years.

There is a statement in historical Latin language texts, "All roads lead to Rome." In America, that was true as well before the interstate highway system was built. Until Interstate 75 was built, all roads led to Cincinnati and Northern Kentucky to get anywhere. The urban cities were the gateways one had to drive through to get to other cities, or to the Midwest or to the South, depending on which way you were headed. The Northern Kentucky urban river cities became orphaned behind tall flood barriers on the one hand and sidestepped again by the location of Interstate 75, built on the edge of the city. Moreover, the roadway was elevated above, over the top of the community—bypassed so to speak. What were our leaders thinking? With less traffic, there was less commerce, and with less commerce, growth all but stalled in the urban sector. The river cities of Covington, Newport, and others suffered and deteriorated over time—until recent years.

Covington is where I was born, grew up, and started a company that today has a national footprint. The Butler family moved to a suburb when I was age 17, and after 38 years, Sue and I returned to the urban area once again to take residency in Domaine de la Rive, a contemporary high-rise condominium we built on the river overlooking the entire skyline. I think my sentimental pride about the city where I grew up and went to school and church, combined with watching our urban fabric deteriorate over the years, fueled a resolve to reverse the momentum and to create a new vibrant center for life and identity in our urban sector. That resolve, more like passion, is what gave rise to the first Towers of Rivercenter in Covington, and seven more buildings, including the residential high-rise named the Ascent, designed by the world-renowned architect Daniel Libeskind.

Life in the Butler Family

I was born into a family that ultimately grew during my lifetime to include eight children, Mom and Dad, and a pet dog, of course. We were raised in a house only 14 blocks back from the Ohio River. It was a tiny place by today's standards, but we were proud of our home—my dad especially. When I drive by 208 Byrd Street today, I wonder how we all fit into little more than 2,300 square feet. Seeing the house brings back sentimental memories, about the alleyways and streets on which I rode my bike, the favorite places for games of hide-and-seek, and the close relationships all of the neighbors enjoyed; we knew all of our neighbors and played as kids together. That is one of the benefits of urban living.

Love was not an emotion nurtured in the Butler household when I was growing up. The word was used sparingly at home, although I knew I was loved. My parents, Robert Mathew Butler and Martha Frances Luschek, lived the realities of the Great Depression. As a result, they intentionally and continuously directed their kids to focus on succeeding, which they perceived to be determined by our religion and values, as well as our financial health. Mom repeatedly warned us: "When you are 18, you are on your own!" I took her seriously and, looking back, I may have been on my own financially from as early as age 14. My sense of urgency, which has served me well through the years, was planted before I was 10 years of age, because I had a visual appreciation for the need to be ready by the time I turned 18.

I am a product of the rich German and Irish Catholic environment that once boasted multiple churches and schools, and brick houses lining the downtown area. I remember those very early years with fondness and a certain pride. We never lacked for food on the table, or shoes and other apparel. We had what we needed. We were taught to be thrifty, to value everything, and to respect everyone. Mom made it clear that we had more than the kids in China, and for that we should be grateful. And we were. We had a good life, albeit pretty simple.

Church was important, rain or shine or snow. Nothing stopped us from getting to church on Sunday. And we kids wouldn't miss it for sure, because when we got home Dad would gather all of us and give us each our Sunday nickel. Each week was like a challenge to see how far that nickel would go in buying penny candy. There was a small store owned by a nice old couple named Glantz and after receiving our weekly nickel, off to Glantz's we would run—I do not ever remember walking—and Mrs. Glantz would patiently and sweetly help us get a small bag of candies. The Sunday nickel was a special treat and when I think back, it is like a revelation to me about where my respect for money, hard work, and well, maybe negotiating (as we did each week at the store) all first began.

While the term love was not often verbally expressed by my parents or amongst my seven siblings, in our own way, we loved each other, and that has grown throughout our adulthood. But everything changed for me at the age of 21, when I had a deep spiritual encounter that has, as per the poet Robert Frost, "made all the difference." Today, I pronounce that I am a person of faith and indeed of love, and as someone frequently labeled as a tough guy, I am unafraid to speak using these terms. Faith and love have always been and remain abundant fuel for my life's work.

My wife, Sue, has helped greatly in this regard, since she grew up in a very tight-knit family and had wonderful role models for forging and sustaining loving relationships. Her family was, in many ways, the polar opposite of ours. In her family, great emphasis was placed on all the siblings being bonded. It seemed to me that was first and foremost. She has brought to our small family the value of those bonds. She is also a person of faith and, like me, has experienced spiritual encounters of a higher order.

Her dad was home each day at 5 p.m. Mine was home each night as well, maybe a little later, but always for dinner at our table for ten. Her dad was a printer, mine owned a substantial plumbing business that did larger commercial projects as I grew up. Her dad was the glue of those bonds. When I delivered his eulogy, I referred to him as the "master of simple fun" and "the instigator of good times." He would create simple games, dice, or puzzles, or cards, bringing everyone in the family together on weekends and holidays.

My dad went into business when he was 22, during the big depression of the 1930s. It was quite difficult to get a steady job during the Great Depression, so he began fixing plumbing for people. And the Robert M. Butler Plumbing Company grew to prominence over the years in Covington and beyond. Dad was well known for his success and entrepreneurial spirit, maybe even more for his generosity and concern for others. He had many close friends, everyone knew him to be a good guy with a good heart, and I could tell, even as a young boy tagging along on errands, that when he met another business guy or politician, they genuinely liked him and respected him.

My dad was a very hard worker. He was up by 6 a.m. to go to work and was home by 5:30 or 6 p.m. to join us for dinner. He started each day in prayer on his knees, and ended each day on his knees next to the bed he would then rest in. He would give thanks to God especially for his health and eyesight. His mother was blind and in a wheelchair with a broken hip for most of the time I was growing up.

Dad's father immigrated to the United States from Ireland, alone, at the age of 17, leaving behind eight brothers and sisters in County Offaly, in central Ireland. Even more incredible, my grandfather on mom's side of the family came all by himself from Germany on a freighter at the young age of 14. Fourteen! Imagine that! When I think of the courage of those two men, I am in awe, and wonder on occasion again if their genes had something to do with what I embarked on at an early age and with regard to the outsized risks I have taken in my path to success. Even today, with fast planes, a trip to another continent falls into the category of adventure. What must it have been like to be 14 years old, to say goodbye to your family so many miles away, knowing you might never see them again, and to head to a place you did not know, or had ever been?! What courage. What desire.

My maternal grandfather was a simple man who delivered milk, at first with horse and buggy. He was a collector of junk, storing everything he came across in a two-stall garage stuffed so full that it was impossible to get inside. The most memorable piece of advice he ever gave me when I was a young boy was, "If someone wants to give you something, take it even if you do not need it. Give it to your next-door neighbor." That concern for others was passed down to my parents, and then to me. Recognizing the value of even small gestures and items stuck with me as well.

In addition to being present for his wife and children, Dad also took care of his mother. He was the sibling motivated and willing to take care of her, and he did, visiting her multiple times each week, and taking one of us children with him. She had gone blind at around age 65 and had been told by doctors that there was nothing that could be done to restore her sight; it was due to hardening of the arteries. But Dad never gave up. He found Dr. Cyril Shrimpf, a Cincinnati eye surgeon who diagnosed cataracts and, when Grandma was 89, took her to a hospital in Cincinnati where she had cataracts from both eyes removed at the same time. To do this back 70 years ago was unheard of. Even today that is not done routinely.

I was there when the bandages were removed, and we pushed her in a wheelchair to the front window on Greenup Street. I remember the "ooh's" and "ah's" as she saw buses when there had been streetcars 25 years earlier, and modern automobiles instead of Model Ts and Packards. She had not seen in more than 20 years! What a gift my dad gave to his mom.

He was also a provider for others in need in our community. Whenever he became aware of someone who lacked basic necessities, he quietly stepped in to give them what they needed, whether it was food, transportation, or sometimes money. His neighbors, our community, were his responsibility, it seemed to me. I respected him tremendously for that caregiver role he seemed very willing to assume, and I hope I have carried his generous legacy forward.

Mom was pretty incredible too. She bore nine children over a period of, say, 13 or 14 years. She also kept all the books and handled the internal business needs for the plumbing business, which was no small feat in itself. Dad also liked to buy property, fix it up, and rent it. She had to keep track of all that—the billings, collections, taxes, and payments. She brought the German school of conduct to the partnership, about saving money, about toughing it out when we got a stomachache, and about succeeding in all things. She was a model of hard work, commitment, and especially of inner strength. To be strong was maybe the most important trait she bred in us. All of my brothers and sisters are indeed successful and strong as a result of her tutorials.

From a young age, my siblings and I all had small jobs to earn our own money, which we stockpiled away for the future. As children, we collected soda bottles and turned them in for pennies a piece. I'd collect objects of metal or newspapers and often pulled a wagonload to the junkyard for cash. But as a family, newspaper recycling was an even bigger deal. My dad had built a large enclosed porch, and we would fill the under-porch space with newspapers, bundling them with twine. When we couldn't fit more newspapers in the cellar, dad would call the junkyard to send a truck over to pick the papers up. Whatever money we earned was ours; he split it up and distributed to his children. We all grew up as big savers and all had piggy banks.

The Depression shaped how we lived, how we ate (cleaning our plates at meals was expected "because children in China are starving," which was, I guess, meant to make us realize how fortunate we were), and how we handled money, which was always to be saved for when we would truly need it.

My earliest memory of my family was when I was around six years old. I was a busy kid, always involved in some activity. I enjoyed school and when at home, I loved building with an erector set. Today it's Legos, back then it was Tinkertoys or, if you were lucky like me, an Erector Set where you could bolt the metal pieces together and even add a pulley and twine with a hook for, say, a hoist. I was good with my hands and took every opportunity to make or build something. That included my own tree house, or platform, really.

There was a single tree in our back yard that went up about 10 feet and then split into a Y. I took two-by-fours and nailed from one side of the Y to the other to build the base for a platform I constructed to sit on. I did this mostly on my own, but, as I look back, it foreshadowed what I would be doing in adulthood: designing and constructing big buildings, changing communities.

My father was enterprising and also loved football, making it clear to me that I should attend St. Xavier High School, also known as St. X, across the river in downtown Cincinnati. My dad wanted his oldest son to attend St. X—because it was in Cincinnati and had a big football team. I was the oldest son by default, as a brother I never knew, my father's namesake Robert, died at age two; he was a twin to my oldest sister. There was a rigid entrance exam to get into St. X, and only the top achievers among applicants are accepted, even today. I was very fortunate to be one of them because my formative experiences at St. Xavier had a huge impact on my future and the person I have become.

The $175 annual tuition my freshman year, 1956, was a lot of money to a one-income family of eight children like ours. My second year, tuition was

$225, then $275, and $325 my senior year. (The tuition is now more than $16,000 per year.)

The standards of performance at St. X were high. As freshmen, we were told that if we did not study four hours after school each day, we would not meet the grade there. I believed the Jesuits, as I believed whatever the clergy told me back then; and for me it was indeed true, I had to study long hours. A typical day, at least during football season, was filled with classes until around 3 o'clock. Since St. X was downtown, we did not have a sports field. We donned shoulder pads and uniforms and rode the school buses to an open field on the river, maybe 40 minutes away, for football practice, then took the bus back downtown, after which I had to get home from school for four hours of studying. There was little time for anything that didn't have to do with school, honestly. My dad was proud that I went to St. X, but fitting football into my schedule was tough and getting good grades was important. For me, failure has never been an option. I had never played football and was not very athletic in those days—and really did not have a burning desire for the game.

Divided Over Football

Unfortunately, practicing for four hours after school, getting back downtown at 6:30–7 p.m. every night, and then finding a way home was interfering with my homework. I was smart, but I wasn't an A student—more like a B or B+ student—and after a few weeks of practice sessions, I knew I had to make a choice. I couldn't play football and still do well in my classes. So I reluctantly quit the team.

I didn't discuss this with my parents, or even alert them that I was having a hard time juggling both football and schoolwork, because I knew it was up to me. My mother had always made that emphatically clear.

Apparently, my dad didn't agree with my choice. Or at least he was much more invested in my being on the team than I had realized. Back in his childhood days, in the late 1920s, he was a big neighborhood football player. Most of his teammates were fellow Irishmen, and he loved the game. In fact, he was proud of the crooked arm he earned after breaking a bone during a game that did not set correctly. It was probably inconceivable that I, his oldest son, wouldn't want to play football—that it wasn't my top priority to stay on the team. That my being on the team was an important point of pride for him was a realization I had too late, not that I would have done anything different.

When I told him I had quit the football team, he was livid. There was apparently a loud exchange—more than a scolding that night. Although I don't remember the event at all, my sister tells me there became a huge breach between us, during which he let me know that he would no longer be paying my tuition if I wasn't going to be on the team. "It was like he wrote you off that night," she said.

I honestly don't remember that night, or the extent of his rage. I am guessing that I must have buried it deeply in my brain—and maybe said to myself: "I will show you." And I think I may have been doing just that for most of my career. We never spoke about it again, though our relationship must have changed. I often referred to the relationship as "stormy."

I decided I had to stay at St. X, even if I had to pay the tuition myself. I believe today that I needed to be there, in that intellectually challenging and highly disciplined environment. To afford tuition the following fall, I withdrew $225 from my credit union account at church, my entire savings, which I had amassed through delivering newspapers on a $4 route during grade school. I think there was a total of $242 in the account. In one fell swoop, it was all but gone. And I was okay with that because it gave me another year at St. X. I regret today disappointing my dad, but my experience at St. X was critical to the person I was to become.

The goal of St. X was to educate and produce strong, courageous changemakers who could make a positive difference in the community. The liberal arts high school was known for preparing many doctors and attorneys, as well as corporate leaders, and some priests. I was unusual in my entrepreneurial interests. Likely shaped by working alongside my entrepreneurial father, I hoped to use my St. X education to succeed as an architect.

I am convinced I would not be successful today if I had not succeeded there first, both intellectually and emotionally. St. Xavier High School turned out to be another one of those poetic events for me "that has made all the difference."

Chapter 2

My Faith Defines Me

The Catholic Church was a constant in my young life. It shaped who I was as a child and who I am as an adult, to some degree. The church where I learned about God and sin, or the avoidance thereof. In many ways, my youth revolved around church, but my life as a Christian began sometime later.

My siblings and I were brought up as traditional Catholics—I attended a Catholic elementary school, St. Mary's Cathedral parish school in Covington, and went on to graduate from St. Xavier High, and then onward to study engineering.

I remember when in grade school I became a "Knight of the Altar," which required special studies to earn medals as I progressed through each level of achievement. Those medals were an important sign that I was growing and succeeding; I actually still have them. We also had a local Boy Scout troop, which I joined. I think the Boy Scouts is a great foundation for young people. I was a board member of the big Dan Beard Council in Cincinnati as an adult, and only recently developed and paid most of the cost of a lodge at the old Camp Powderhorn, where I went as a young scout. I love the Scout Law: A Scout is trustworthy, loyal, helpful, friendly, courteous, kind, obedient, cheerful, thrifty, brave, clean, and reverent. We should imbue every young man and woman too with such character foundation.

My experience at St. X was a huge pivot point in my life. The Jesuit motto is "Men for Others." Isn't it interesting how so few words can mean so much and be so lasting?! The Jesuits' mission, as I was told by one of the priests later, is to get into the heads of bright guys, often from well-to-do families, during their teens, with an eye for how to shape the future. They did that by challenging students intellectually and in every way on an almost constant basis. Education at St. Xavier was more than textbook.

In fact, looking back, learning intellectually was maybe only 50 percent of what I gained in those four years. It was all about spirited conversation, debate, studying leaders like Julius Caesar, Jesus Christ, the martyrs. Making us stretch our minds. We were often asked to consider, for example, "Could I be a martyr?" And questions like, "Does the end justify the means, or does the means justify the end?" The Jesuit tradition was to teach students what it meant to be a leader, what leaders looked like, how they made a difference, and how they were able to change the world, in the hopes that students themselves would go out into the world and make a difference. It was a highly disciplined environment, often with rules that did not make sense—again, not until one looks back over many years. Then I came to realize what St. Xavier and the Jesuits had to do with my formation, purpose in life, and confidence too—maybe even risk taking.

During high school, I also had my first deeply spiritual experience. I remember it clearly, even decades later. I was 17 and in my second-floor bedroom of our family's house, doing my homework at my desk after school when, all of a sudden, I felt such strong emotions that I started to tear up. It lasted maybe 30 seconds and although I wasn't sure what had brought those feelings on, I knew I had been in the presence of a higher order. What I had experienced I can only describe as pure love.

Later in life, I spoke with priests and religious leaders to try to better understand that fleeting experience and I was assured that with God, "You know. You know when it happens." Even as a teenager, I knew.

I like to also refer to these high school years as the idealistic period in my life. Those years were the height of idealism, probably because they were, to me, the romantic period as well, when I set my goals for the woman I would marry. I did that by seeking to meet her in every good young lady I met. And I knew more than a few over time, and dated more than a few, because that is what my wise mother always told me to do: "play the field."

I fell in love more than once, and wrote poetry as an expression, not just when emotionally shook, but as an expression of who I was, and who I wanted to be. I was 15 when I wrote my first poem, not about my own problem but about my good friend Paul's hurt feelings over a romantic relationship. Of all the poems I wrote, two of them always stuck with me as sentimental favorites, with "Younger Years" being the first.

Younger Years

The younger years, the wilder years
The Lover's Tears, the Childish fears
These and more are but a few things that
This mad growing up brings

A love so true, a love so mad
In a few months they go away sad
But only shortly last the tears
For these are the younger years.

You are sad and you are lonely
But time flies and you are not the only
Youngster momentarily with tears
For these are the younger years.

Ages will come and roll along
And years from now many will sing this same song
Young lovers cry and who hears
For these are the younger years.

Life has always been the same
And who can be picked to blame
But in the end dark turns to clear
For these are the younger years.

I wrote my favorite poem sometime later, called "Supernatural Nature." It was a perfect iambic pentameter as poetry goes. I was clearly searching, reaching, visioning about what it is all about, this life, these emotions. It was a cool work of expression in which I took pride.

Supernatural Nature

It's sometimes hard explaining those things
We feel down deepest underneath
Those words we manage
Though they seem
To be exactly what we mean
Depending on the times we speak
Can be untrue and very weak.

To these things we think and hesitate
And beat our brains and self to hate
Remembering that this much is true
The nature in and around I and you
Accepted by all, realized and named
Cannot possibly be explained.

Signs Emerge

To pay my high school tuition for my junior and senior years, I worked three part-time jobs: as a busboy at a notable restaurant named Olsner's, delivering brooms made by the blind to their customers, and packaging imported tea for distribution by an English doctor. I also had a full-time summer job in the warehouse at Kruse Hardware for two summers in a row, between my junior and senior years and between graduating from high school and entering Ohio

College of Applied Science, which had recently become a part of the University of Cincinnati.

Although we weren't as close as we might have been, my dad and I were still father and son, and I enjoyed working with him and learning about the plumbing trade. I even operated a backhoe excavator and loader for him in the summertime during high school. I was only 14 or 15 years old at that point and yet drove the equipment on the streets. That was allowed because it was classified a farm tractor, not a vehicle, and there was no license required for that. But then another pivotal event occurred during my senior year of high school. Some things you remember in vivid detail.

It was after school one day. I was cleaning up Dad's shop, labelling and putting pipe fittings into bins, when he came into the room and at the top of his voice said, "This is my company and you're not going to take it from me!"

I was 16 or 17 and utterly confused by my dad's sense that I was trying to take over his business. I wasn't exactly sure what to do, so I went to Father McKenna, my counselor at St. X, for advice. I told him, "I do not know if my dad wants me to be in the plumbing business. What should I do?"

He asked me, in turn, "What do you want to do?"

"I always wanted to be an architect," I told him, "but that would not be right for the plumbing business." He directed me to look into a new college that had just been started by the University of Cincinnati. It was an intense engineering school that led to an associate's degree, which could be in civil engineering—perfect preparation for the plumbing business, he told me. Then, he said, "If you still do not know the answer after graduating there, then continue on, finish up at the University of Cincinnati campus in architecture."

Understanding My Dad

Back then, as I struggled to decide between my dad's plumbing business and a career in architecture, my dad was enduring a private struggle of his own. It wasn't until many years later that I figured out that, at the time of these incidents, Dad was in the early stages of Alzheimer's disease. But in the 1950s, Alzheimer's had not been discovered nor labelled as such. The doctor called it "little strokes."

When we look back over many years of progress in defining Alzheimer's disease, there is no doubt about Dad's symptoms. Alzheimer's caused his extreme behavior. The emotional events he started having when he was only 50 or 51, accompanied by occasional dizziness, were symptoms of the disease that would later take his life at far too early an age. I know he would not have said those things to me—lost his cool—if it were not for the disease. I have no doubt. But in the end, it set my course in life and, in hindsight, it must have been meant to be. He never saw the buildings we built or the fruits of the counsel he often gave me during car rides together.

Dad passed away approximately nine years later after his first symptoms, at only 59.

But Mom saw what we did at Corporex. She was always game to go up those rickety construction elevators to survey the tall buildings we built, even when there were no walls at all. She got to ride on the Goodyear Blimp once, when the Goodyear pilots offered to give me a ride as part of my contract for building a huge hangar in Pompano Beach, Florida, that housed two blimps at the same time. I flew Mom and Kevin and Christa and Sue to Florida; we were even allowed to sit in the captain's seat to steer and fly the big dirigible. Mom never forgot that trip up and down the coast of Florida, along the beaches in the blimp; and I have never forgotten her excitement. How many of her friends ever did that?! Indeed, she witnessed much of my success and lived to the age of 91.

My Roots in Construction

Ultimately, I studied structural engineering at Ohio College of Applied Science (OCAS), the UC-affiliated school Father McKenna had recommended to me, and by the time I finished my associate's degree, I had a big desire to design and build buildings; the plumbing business did not appeal to me any longer. My middle brother, Mike, took Butler Plumbing forward, protecting and enhancing the Robert M. Butler Plumbing name for years very successfully. So, again, it appears in retrospect that those two events, those encounters with Dad, they set my course in life, and that, too, was likely providential. It was meant to be, again, I think in ways guided.

Immediately after graduating from engineering school, in late 1962, I marched up to the University of Cincinnati (UC) to sign up for the next three years to get my bachelor's degree in architecture, only to be disappointed. The registrar's office told me I would have to start over as a first-year student, because UC did not accept the credits from their affiliated college because OCAS used a different curriculum. It's unlikely such university rigidness would be the policy now, but back then, I was out of luck. The advice I had received when I enrolled at OCAS was incorrect and it would have taken me five more years to earn a bachelor's degree.

As a result of not having a bachelor's degree, I second-guessed myself a lot initially. However, eventually I came to the conclusion that between my high school education at St. X and my college studies at OCAS, scholastically, I'd had the equivalent of a college education. However, that still didn't change how I felt about myself. If I could, I would go back and get that college degree if only for the confidence it would have given me.

I decided that was not the best use of my time and getting a job was a better next step. It wasn't in my nature to start over; I only wanted to keep moving forward. I was an impatient young man and wanted to get on with life. I never did get that architecture degree, but over the years I have had as many as a dozen architects at one time on my payroll. Even to this day, we design and shape most of the buildings we build and develop for ownership ourselves. Being the visionary that I am known to be, I have the privilege of adding my ideas and directions to those designs and the pleasure of knowing that design features and concepts, even shapes, were at my direction and sourced in my brain.

Since I had been working as a co-op student for a German contractor named Al Lubrecht during college, when my plan to attend UC fell through, I turned to him to ask if he might have a full-time job for me. He did, and I started officially in January 1963.

Essentially, I worked as an engineer for him, but I also worked in the field, supervised crews, hung steel, and operated heavy equipment, too. Mr. Lubrecht became an important mentor to me, for which I am so grateful. Thanks to him and his trust in me and my abilities, I learned the construction business from working in the field, rather than sitting in an office; I learned it from the bottom up. The training at OCAS was top-notch and 90 percent of what I was taught was engineering-related, so I began work for Mr. Lubrecht with a strong foundation in the field, even if it wasn't a bachelor's degree. He then supplemented what I had learned in my classes with real-life experience from day one.

Where most architecture students learn the basics in class and then have to figure out how to apply them in the field, I learned by doing. I learned how to draw buildings as if I were an architect. These were industrial buildings. I also did the engineering layout work for buildings throughout Cincinnati and Kentucky. I drew the plan for a US Shoe Corporation warehouse building, for example, and I observed first-hand how to deliver service at a high level. Back then, one didn't always need a certified engineer to review and approve drawings, or a stamp signifying approval. That's how I could prepare drawings that were used in construction.

Nate Stix, CEO of US Shoe, would call and say, "Al, we want to put a manufacturing building on this piece of land we own in Flemingsburg, Kentucky." Most of Mr. Lubrecht's clients trusted him without question and he did the work without a written contract. That was then, those were different times. Later, at Corporex, we always wrote comprehensive contracts that spelled out the understanding and what we would deliver. We did it to build a foundation for a long-term relationship like those that Mr. Lubrecht had with his clients. In retrospect, I wonder if that is where it began—my earnest quest to build long-term relationships with customers and others in business. I witnessed the way Mr. Lubrecht valued integrity, above all else I think, and being somewhat idealistic myself, I wanted that too.

I did not design all the buildings that Mr. Lubrecht did, but I did some. I also supervised as many as 30 laborers at one point on work in the Newport Steel Plants in the early '60s. For more than two years, until March 15, 1965, I worked closely with Mr. Lubrecht. But by late 1964, early 1965, I felt I was ready—ready to take the big leap. We both knew that there wasn't much upward mobility possible in his small firm since his goal was to pass on the business to his son Joe, who was my friend and schoolmate. It was actually through his son that I happened to meet Mr. Lubrecht. And the truth is, from the outset, I was destined to be my own boss.

Although he probably thought I was a little crazy for striking out on my own at such a young age, Mr. Lubrecht was encouraging and supportive. Indeed, he was my mentor, my coach. We would often sit on Saturday morning in his office—me in a big, overstuffed chair, and he in his leather high-back—and we would talk, talk, talk, about me a lot, about dreams and desires, about the important things in a young man's life. He was a good mentor, good teacher, and I know he liked to do this for people like me. I must have intrigued him in those days, I must have had big dreams to share, lofty goals, and a lot of naivete I am sure. If I had to pick one word that described Al Lubrecht, it is "wise." He was a wise man, also a man of God. In many ways, he helped me prepare for the challenging career that lay in front of me.

I remember one time, as I shared my impatience while riding in a car with him, he told me, "Don't confuse impatience with ambition." I never forgot those few words or the exact street intersection where they were spoken. He knew I was ambitious and he supported me. So, when I told him I would leave to enter business, he wished me well.

Before I took the leap to become self-employed, I did a short stint in the U.S. Army Reserves. In those days every young man who was able-bodied was required to serve time in one of the branches of the military. I think that should still be the case today, because I look at this experience with fondness. I learned a lot. I needed to get this obligation behind me. ER15671501. That is who I was, a number, and those were my call signs. I never forget a number. Being impatient, I elected to go to the enlisted Army Reserves, which required six months up front and six years of weekends and summer camps thereafter to conclude my obligation.

Mr. Lubrecht's son and I had set up a dummy supply company together, called B&L Supply, as a way to get around the prohibition the plywood companies had against selling to contractors. Wholesalers, like Weyerhaeuser or

US Plywood, wouldn't sell directly to a contractor. To protect the wholesalers' relationship with the lumberyards, they required contractors to buy their plywood at the lumberyard. So we formed a company that Weyerhaeuser and US Plywood recognized as a supplier vendor, which allowed us to buy direct. We could then mark the plywood up and sell it to contractors.

When I left Mr. Lubrecht to go into business for myself, he let me take that business with me, probably because I had been the one keeping the records and paying the bills. That was a lifesaver when I was getting started, because I could go drive to homebuilders in the area for example and ask if they needed any plywood.

Chapter 3

A Huge Need to Succeed

A drive to succeed in every aspect of my life has served me well. I realize in retrospect how involved I was in both church and community, even when I was in high school and college. I was asked to be a member of the first-ever Urban Renewal Advisory Committee for the City of Covington when I was 18. I was elected president of the Cathedral Holy Name Society at age 20, which was a surprise to me, and likely to others. No one that age had ever led such an important church organization. I wasn't sure I was ready, but I was proud that others had confidence in me, and I took it on.

The Holy Name Society was more than 300 members strong, all men at that time, most of whom were older than I was by at least 20 to 40 years. These were the community movers and shakers, as well as the fathers of many of my early years' classmates. My father took me to Sunday meetings as a young boy, and I was proud to become a member in my teens. We met monthly for Sunday mass, followed by a hearty breakfast, at which notable speakers often addressed the group. A couple names I recall were George Ratterman and Charlie Keating, who spoke on their Citizens for Decent Literature efforts, but there were multiple dignitaries who spoke at our Sunday breakfasts. On top of education and congregation, the Holy Name Society also did good works in the community, including putting up an impressive nativity scene, complete with a large building and live animals, held a big parade down Madison Avenue to open the nativity season, as well as sponsoring the most popular youth dance every Saturday night in the school Lyceum. Students came from far and wide to attend those dances.

When I look back on those years, I get the picture that I was somewhat of an activist even then, and maybe even a leader of sorts. My position as president of the Holy Name Society led to my being asked by the pastor of the Cathedral parish to represent the parish at the first men's spiritual weekend, called Cursillo. I had no idea how during this weekend my life would be forever changed.

The Cursillo is a movement within the Catholic Church, as well as within many Christian congregations under different names and styles. The word Cursillo is Spanish and means "a Little Course in Christianity." A bishop in Majorca, Spain, founded the weekends as a way to get men back to church—and somehow the movement jumped over to the United States, thanks to the Franciscans. The weekends are conducted mostly by laypersons, and some clergy, but mostly it is a lay movement to foster Christianity at an apostolic energy level. Unlike most retreats, this one involves an extra day, 15 talks, and lots of discussion on the topics, and resolutions in the end. Upon arrival, we were told that we were "called" by the Holy Spirit, and that is why we found ourselves there for the weekend.

When My Life In God Began Anew

Throughout the weekend I attended, we candidates were challenged by, among other questions, this question: "Would you turn your whole self over to Christ?" "Would you answer the call?" Sunday came, and we were advised there would be a closing ceremony so, for me, that meant time was running out to answer that question. I found that for most of the other men, there was not such urgency; the levels of commitment varied. For me, it was different. I needed to pray over this question.

Alone in a dark chapel with only a flickering candle, I knelt at the railing, and prayed, and prayed—and I crossed a line of no return when I said somehow, down deep, "I do."

What happened when I crossed that line of commitment is something that many men are reluctant to tell, at least not in the way I will describe it. But I have to tell, because it was real, and it was life altering, and again, it made all the difference in my entire future from that point forward. Here is what I experienced and recall vividly even to this moment. There was like an explosion in my brain, bright light—brilliant light. I experienced something that I had never known before or since. It is difficult to describe in such a way as people who have not been there can comprehend. I was filled with overwhelming energy, and joy, and love, and peace—and importantly, all at the same time, all four elements, and all simultaneously. It was indeed a turning point in this young man's person, and journey.

It was 3:30 in the afternoon on, Sunday, October 11, 1964. It was incredible and, to this day, 58 years later, I still possess in my mind that wall of light, the same brilliant light that I experienced that Sunday afternoon. It never goes away, recedes until something or some conversation causes me to recall that moment and then it immediately returns. It is a constant reminder to me about God, the Source of all life, and that there are indeed souls, spirits so to speak, active in our lives, and close at hand, present. It took many years of looking back on my life to understand the meaning, the significance, of what happened on October 11, 1964 at that very moment. For at least 20 years, when I looked back over my life, I could not see anything of my personal life beyond that moment in time, beyond the wall of light. Finally, with some help of family members, I did recover memories, at least in part, about my earlier years that I had not been able to recall. Otherwise, I could not share my story and career fully about the formative years, or those that followed.

I discovered what happened to me was what the Protestants always talked about—"to be born again." The explosion of light was a demarcation point in my life. It was a born-again encounter with Christ. It was when my life in God began anew, and I was fueled with the energy, the Spirit, deeper purpose, and a new and full dimension of love, and understanding of love in its many dimensions. I hope I have been true to that moment, that encounter, in my work, in my personal development, in my life.

My Entrepreneurial Start

Five months after that profound spiritual experience, in March of the following year, I spent my first days as an entrepreneur, in a small one-room office, as I embarked upon creating what is now Corporex. The plan to go on my own was solidified following the spiritual experience—I was committed to self-employment—but now I had a new potential problem: how to deal with the conflict between apostleship and capitalism.

The impact of my spiritual experience on Corporex has been huge and is why we sometimes refer to Corporex as being "more than a financial enterprise," as we have tried to weave these core Christian tenets and commitment into our corporate framework, our very mission and purpose, including both our internal and external environment. Once again, "that has made all the difference."

Humble Beginnings

My dad had a nice plumbing business building complex—not small by any standard, with multiple buildings. He had built a five-stall garage at the rear of the yard. When I embarked on my own, Dad let me set up shop in one of those garage bays. I took the overhead door out and put a door and window in, plus a ceiling overhead and laid a linoleum floor over the concrete. I built a drawing board myself out of plywood, bought a four-dollar desk from the St. Vincent de Paul thrift store, as well as a used typewriter. Thanks to an optional class I had taken at St. X in my sophomore year, I could type better than most people.

I also had a phone and the damn thing never rang. I remember my thinking even to this day: "Butler, what have you done ?!" I was very fearful and scared about the unknown I had jumped into.

With each passing day, I became more anxious, but I kept my routine. As a result of my profound spiritual experience, I went to church every day at 6 a.m. That's where I started my day, and I'd get to work at 7. On my first day in business, I had $20 in my billfold and two weeks later, I still had most of that $20, which tells me that I must have poached a lot of drinks or cigarettes during those first weeks. Back then, everyone smoked, including me. Clearly, I was holding on to every penny I had, scared, realizing that building a business was going to be harder than I had imagined.

The pressure I felt was all about success, about being successful, for me. Money wasn't a motivator at that time, although I knew that money was essential to success if such was to be accomplished in the business world. My upbringing, the challenges presented by my dad and mom, the encouragement of Mr. Lubrecht, and my recent spiritual encounter had brought me to this point and collectively fueled me with boundless energy and determination.

I didn't yet have grand ideas for what my company could do or be in the future because I was so focused then on figuring out how to make a go of it. Landing work at the time was my only aim.

I immediately realized that I had never actually built a building, had never signed a contract to do so; I was only one person in the organizational structure in A. J. Lubrecht Construction Company that accomplished those things. But, whoa, this was different now that I was in charge and on my own.

My creativity must have kicked in at the time, as I wracked my brain for how to make money as an entrepreneur. I'm sure my fear of failure helped, too. I set out to sell building materials to whoever would buy from me, as a way to get enough money to live on week to week.

Once in the office at 7 a.m. after daily mass, I would begin typing direct mail letters to send out to contractors, mainly, as well as to local architects and other folks in the business, to try to persuade them to buy what I had to offer. My original expectation at that time was that I was going to start out building smaller buildings, like service stations, which were springing up all over the place back in the mid-1960s. Because they were small, I thought I could get contracts to build them. I figured that I might have to work my way up to getting contracts for larger, more complex buildings. Never mind that I had never built a building myself, but I thought people would let me try. But the truth is, at the age of 22, I was not ready to undertake even a $40,000 contract like a service station. I lacked the people, the experience, and the reputation for having done it successfully.

Being in a small community, every businessperson there knew that I had never built a building. There was no denying it or talking around it. And few executives were going to trust a construction job to a man who had never built a building on his own, I soon learned.

What had I done?!

Why in the world had I thought that I could just quit my job at the age of 22 and somebody was going to give me a contract to build a building, when I'd never done it before on my own. I didn't have a balance sheet, didn't have a financial statement, and didn't have months of emergency funds set aside. It was what you'd call at a minimum, blind ambition. But more like crazy, as I think back.

I must have started W. P. Butler Company with less than $1,000 in total worth to my name, which I had saved following graduation from college in late 1962. That included my car and the truck I had rebuilt. I know for sure it was not more than that. I had put in a stint in the army also for six months in 1963, so my entire worth was what I had saved after working essentially two and a half years at an average wage of $2.50 per hour. I must have thought $1,000 was a good nest egg, and within a couple of months I began to wonder if I had made a big mistake. In hindsight, I probably looked ridiculous.

One day, a larger local homebuilder named Ralph Drees, with whom I became close friends later in life, gave me a small order for two dozen pieces of a particular kind of plywood. With that contract in-hand, I drove my car back to the office, got out of my shirt and tie, put on my work clothes, jumped into my truck and headed over to pick up the plywood at the distribution center, then took it back over to the job site. Within three hours, the plywood had been delivered. Best service in town!

This became a common routine, after which I'd head back to the office, change back into my shirt and tie, and head back out to sell some more. From 8 a.m. until dusk, probably, I would be out knocking on doors to drum up some business, or at least a relationship.

My Next Bold Decision

When I started the business, my brother-in-law helped me keep my company's income and expenses straight by acting as my bookkeeper, because I expected that I would soon be so busy that I wouldn't have time to devote to such matters. I certainly didn't lack self-confidence, did I?! Well, about seven months later, I stopped by his home for an end-of-month update, and he told me that I had only $200 remaining in the company's bank account. I was effectively broke. I was stunned. Was I at the end of my entrepreneurial career already?

I felt numb. Failure felt sad and lonely, but I couldn't quite accept it.

It was a long drive home, even though the distance was a short six miles. My impending failure was the only thing on my burdened mind. From the outset, one of my deep pledges was to make the business more than a one-dimensional financial enterprise. Reminding myself of that vision, I was filled with faith and buoyed with confidence. I came to a bold decision.

All who were alive when John F. Kennedy was shot remember exactly where they were the moment they heard the news. Well, that night was similarly momentous for me. I remember the exact place where I was when I made my big decision.

As I drove home, likely praying, I came up to the stop sign on Crescent Street in Covington. It is in the middle of the block, where the road jogs sharply. I knew what I needed to do.

I went home and wrote a check to the church, I do not recall exactly what recipient, in the amount of $100—half of my entire cash remaining. I put the check in an envelope, put a stamp on it, and mailed it first thing in the morning on my way to work. I was confident that giving that money away was the right course of action. It was meant as an expression of my deep faith.

The next day I walked into the Covington Trust Bank and introduced myself to a loan officer named Bill Rolf. I explained that I would soon be getting orders coming in, and I had a contract to build a friend's home addition as well, so I needed some capital in order to make it to the other end. I was all of

22 with seven months of business experience behind me, but Mr. Rolf took a chance on me. He gave me a $2,500 loan on my signature and a promise to repay within 90 days.

Well, some of those orders did come in, though I do not recall the specifics, and somehow, exactly 89 days later, I did repay it.

And I have mused over time that I took a walk around the block, reentered the bank, and asked Bill Rolf for a $5,000 loan this time. I've been doing that ever since, borrowing larger amounts of money, repaying, and borrowing more.

That money was critical at the time and without that original small loan, I would have been out of business. Desperate to make some money, and with the prospects of building buildings remote, I began investigating new income streams and landed on manufacturers' representatives as an avenue to explore. I remember spending lots of time at the Cincinnati library to research architectural product manufacturers that used representatives to sell their products. There was the *Encyclopedia of Architectural Products*, which I became very familiar with. I focused on structural building systems because my structural engineering education naturally leaned toward building systems, and I understood those components. After taking copious notes on the companies listed that used manufacturers' reps, I went back to my office and typed up letters asking for authorization to represent them. As a manufacturer's representative, I did not need money except for my costs of living. For every one of their products I sold, I would earn a small commission, and I saw this as a way to stay alive, to generate some income. Since there was little downside to adding me as a representative, companies began approving me; they didn't know I was only 22. And I started having some success.

I sold bar joist, which was a structural roof system. Then I sold laminated wood structures for a company named Laminated Rafters, Inc. in Baton Rouge, Louisiana. Laminated wood is a wood product that has been glued together into a shape, such as a structural arch for a church. I was successful selling those types of products into the construction industry because I could lean on my structural engineering knowledge. Then I found a company that manufactured pre-engineered metal buildings, which, back then, was a relatively new concept.

Although pre-engineered buildings represent 60 percent of the industrial buildings that are built today, then they were considered cheap and undesirable. Many of the products I represented were leading edge, which meant they were a challenge for me to sell, because they hadn't yet caught on and buyers weren't very receptive to them. On the other hand, being on the leading edge gave me a distinctive position on which to advance and persuade.

My luck began to change after I became a distributor for a business that was smaller and evolving: American Buildings Company. American Buildings Company was very small then, less than $10 million in annual sales, and didn't have the financing to expand into the North by setting up their own satellite offices or sales force. So they designated intermediary distributors to represent the company initially, in the mid-America states. There were about five of us distributors just in the northern part of the country, and we were responsible for finding contractors and making them franchised dealers. The dealers would then work to get contracts to design and build a building using American Buildings Company's materials. As the middleman, I earned a 4 percent commission on each sale.

Being extremely ambitious, and in need of cash, I took on all of Ohio, Kentucky, and West Virginia myself. It was a huge territory, looking back, and I was determined to make the most of the opportunity. Fairly quickly, I had contractor dealers in Cincinnati, Columbus, and Dayton as well as in Louisville, even Cleveland, and as far away as Paducah, Kentucky.

That meant I put a lot of miles on my second-hand cars—as many as 100,000 in any one year—mainly because I was willing to drive anywhere to quote a project. I was so committed to making the sale, even when driving wasn't necessarily the most efficient use of my time, that I would travel to customers to seal the deal. One time I drove to Prestonsburg, Kentucky (nearly 200 miles away), got a signed order for a pre-engineered building from a prominent mining contractor in 45 minutes and then drove home immediately. That remains my fastest sale ever. Often, I would provide engineering for foundations and other support to my contractors in order for them to estimate and bid on the work. Most of them could only build, but had no design or engineering skills, so I often drew the plans and sized the foundations for the building on which they would compile a cost estimate and bid to give to the customer. I could stretch a dollar well back then.

Once the dealer landed the contract, I would sell them the metal building and get my commission, which wasn't huge given all the work I had done. A big order would have been $40,000–$60,000 tops, and I would receive all of $1,600, or $2,000 for my part, although most of the projects were smaller than that. Back then this was important money, and I, with low, low overhead, could pay my bills mostly on time.

Pre-engineered metal buildings, being a newer concept, used lighter metal components, and required a different type of tradesman, and the usual trade workers who erected steel simply were not trained to do this work. When they did try, they did it poorly. Getting the metal buildings erected in a quality way was the biggest problem my dealers had. So I solved it for them.

Because I had learned how to erect steel and manage and supervise ironworkers, thanks to my experience with heavy iron and concrete while working with A. J. Lubrecht Construction Company, I ended up employing and training erection crews to install the buildings. That meant that I was designing the foundations and the buildings for the dealers, as well as building the primary structures. At one point I had eight erection crews running, we were so busy.

Later, as we evolved into a turnkey operation, I would design and construct entire buildings, which was my original goal. I was already doing the hard work and gaining a lot of confidence in my own ability, and building a small level of working capital too.

Chapter 4

It's All About Love

I was already in business, a single man, when I met the lady I would marry.

My mother always told me to "play the field," meaning, to get to know as many girls as I could before deciding which one I might want to marry. I took her advice to heart during high school and college. I was a social guy and dated many girls, as was typical of that era. That usually meant going to a Saturday night dance at the Cathedral School Building in Covington, or a Sunday dance at St. John's. Once in a while, we might go to the movies or to a school event or party, but the church dances were the primary places you could socialize with friends and meet girls.

The point of dating in those years was simply to get to know one another. It was truly a social activity, nothing more. One way to do that was to offer a girl a ride home after a dance, so that you'd have a chance to talk.

I enjoyed getting to know people—still do—so I was a regular at local events and get-togethers, frequently pulling up in my dad's pickup truck, which was emblazoned with the "Butler Plumbing" name on the side. For a long time, the Butler Plumbing truck was the only transportation I had; Dad would only let me use the family Chevrolet for a prom event. I always voiced that the pickup truck became an early test for girls I took on dates. If I pulled up to their home in that pickup truck and they were still willing to go out with me, and then said yes to a second date later; well then that was an indicator that they were of good character. They didn't care about the type of car I drove.

I think I always knew I would get married someday, but around the age of 19 or 20, I decided that I would resist the temptation to do so should the occasion rise. Actually, I made a promise to myself that I wouldn't get married until I was age 26. I wanted a family, but I had other things I wanted to accomplish before I settled down and took on that responsibility.

I was very logical about the whole process and things were going well on that front, until I met Mary Sue Lutz and fell head-over-heels in love.

The Ideal Girl

It was at a dance for singles in Cincinnati sponsored by the Jack and Jill club, which was an organization for single adults. I had attended half a dozen Jack and Jill dances held at various locations around the city and typically featured a disc jockey. The dances were always well-attended, and there would be at least 200 people or so there. I loved to dance, and thanks to my sisters having taught me how to jitterbug, I was pretty good at it.

This particular dance was held at a VFW hall and I went with two friends of mine; we drove together over to Cincinnati. We mingled for a bit, but as soon as Sue walked in the front door, she caught my eye. She was smiling, chatting with people casually, and I couldn't help notice the aura around her. Trust me, there seemed to be a glow, and I couldn't take my eyes off of her. I wanted to ask her to dance, but it took me almost the whole night to summon the courage. When I finally did, it was the second-to-last dance.

Thankfully, she said yes, and we seemed to connect. The last call was a slow dance, and we stayed on the floor to dance to that. Being afraid I would not see her again unless I took action, I offered to drive her home and, wow, she said yes.

A few days later, I called to ask her on a date and she turned me down. I have to admit, I was surprised. We had gotten along so well. Undeterred, I called again the following week to ask her out and this time she said yes.

Several months into our relationship, the Jack and Jill club sponsored a ski trip to Michigan. Sue was going with her friends, so I decided I would, too. The fact that neither of us knew how to ski did not deter us from having this adventure. And it was on that trip that we both became closer. From then on, I think we were exclusive, but there was no formal agreement or discussion about such a status.

Not long after the ski trip, I encouraged Sue to attend a Cursillo weekend, similar to what I had attended about 18 months before. I was her official sponsor for the weekend, which she attended with her girlfriend as part of the very first women's Cursillo weekend in the Diocese. The weekend I had attended had been one of the very first men's Cursillo retreats. And, like me, she had a profound spiritual encounter there—not the same as mine, not as impactful, but for her, very moving.

After the Cursillo weekend, we were that much more bonded and sure of our path forward together. As I reflect, I recognize now that we were both so committed to Christ, but also committed to each other at that point. Sue always says that if she had not made that Cursillo weekend, I would not have married her. I cannot say that she was right, but, well, I cannot say she was wrong either. But after her weekend our relationship was for sure changed.

Our courtship was not typical, at least by comparison to my friends' dates. Our outings almost always began at church, in the chapel, where we prayed together at the altar rail, and then we headed out to the movies or a dance. Otherwise, it was like any other young couple at that time. We went to movies, or out to dinner, especially at the White Horse Tavern to celebrate whenever I secured a contract in my business. It did not matter the size of the deal I signed, but it was another good excuse to take her out and be with her. We spent a lot of time with our families, especially hers, and with our friends, hanging out at bars, or bowling alleys sometimes, where we all gathered.

Since I had decided years before that I would not marry before age 26, I was in no rush to make our relationship permanent, though by that point I knew Sue was the one.

Eighteen months before we married, she went on a three-week trip to Europe with a church group and I got a taste of what life without Sue was like. I still remember watching her plane take off and the awful feeling in my stomach. It told me everything.

The adage that "absence makes the heart grow fonder" was never more true for me, and as soon as she returned home, we talked seriously, and not too many months thereafter became engaged. We were married on February 24, 1968, when I was 25 and she 23.

Our wedding day was special to us, as I'm sure wedding days are special for everyone, but this was not a wedding just of us to each other, but of three to the other, including that One I today call the Light. There is no question, God was at the center of our vows on that day. We always knew that we were not alone when we faced many stresses and challenges together, because we were three from that time forward.

Over time, I have learned, love is like a kaleidoscope: it keeps unfolding and revealing as we turn on the life journey. That has been fuel to me these last 50-plus years. And love is the fuel of my spouse as well.

Somewhere in my high school years I had written another poem named "The Ideal Girl," and painted in my mind an idealistic picture of that person I sought. It is clear to me that I found her, and 55 years of marriage has proven that Sue was the one, the ideal girl for me, the one who was hidden in the picture.

Putting Down Roots

Sue's and my first home was a two-bedroom apartment in the upstairs portion of a building that had been divided into two units, one up and one down. I went into business in 1965, we married in 1968, and in 1969 I signed a contract to buy my first industrial park property. To accomplish my vision, I borrowed a huge amount of money to do so; I personally signed the guarantee, and Sue did too. The monthly payments on that land were $1,003 plus 80 cents, exactly, whereas our apartment cost all of $115 per month. That surely gave Sue some angst about the guy she married; "He just hocked our whole life with a huge loan that transcends numbers not ever imagined when he married me"—by either of us for that matter.

However, I did not dally long to get her a home of her own, by borrowing more money and beginning the design and construction of our first house, in a new subdivision called Twelve Trees. It was a 2,450-square-foot ranch-style with three bedrooms. I drew the plans and constructed it and furnished it within 12 weeks, so that we could move in one year after the purchase of the business park land. It was a great neighborhood of younger couples and we developed friends for life from the frequent get-togethers of that time.

It was almost three years after we married that our children came along—first Kevin, and later Christa, and the two of them completed our family.

Kevin was an active baby who seemed destined to have a career in sports. At one and a half years, just beginning to talk, he asked for a "feetball" (also known as a football) for Christmas. It was the only gift he truly wanted that year and was ecstatic to receive it. Sports were in his genes and he excelled at all that he tried.

After playing several sports in school, he attended Drake University, majoring in communications with an emphasis in advertising, and went on to work at famed advertising agency Leo Burnett in Chicago. Sports then pulled him to work at ESPN next, and then back to the Cincinnati area, where he now is building youth soccer programs around the country. He has two boys, Logan and Connor, and they are exciting guys to witness as they develop.

Christa was born two years after Kevin and also excelled at everything she did, including sports. She was a champion sprinter on top of being a brilliant student. After earning her degree in psychology from Xavier University, cum laude no less, she went on to earn a master's in education from John Carroll University.

Now settled in Northern California, Christa taught elementary school for many years and was a favorite of students and administrators alike, because she could teach multiple subjects and go wherever she was needed. Today she is a talented playwright. She has two teenagers, Frida and Johannes. They, too, are smart and capable and their potential to make a difference is also exciting.

Since their birth, Kevin and Christa have brought love and fulfillment to their parents' lives. Their children, too, make their grandparents very happy.

Part II

Builder—of Buildings, of Companies

"The corporate career is only the undercarriage to a fascinating life journey."

—WILLIAM P. BUTLER

Chapter 5

Finding My Seat at the Table

The challenge I faced in the early days of business was that I was a 20-something young man who was known in the community, and whose lack of building experience was also acknowledged. It wasn't so much that I was well-known, but my dad was, and being a relatively small population center, people knew well that I was Bob Butler's young son. Yes, I like to think I was respected, but no company in my local community would hire my business to construct buildings because they knew I had never done it. My problem was proximity. I also had a problem with a dealer account in Louisville who had gotten upset with American Buildings Company, the manufacturer I represented.

To solve both problems, I had an unconventional idea. (My solution ended up earning me the coveted National Entrepreneur of the Year award three decades later.)

Northern Kentucky, at the time, had only 130,000 residents. Every business person in town knew without asking that I, a young person in his early 20s had never built a building. Not only that, but I was asking them to give me a contract to include both design and construction of their building. That was unconventional in those days, but now it is acceptable. I was one of the pioneers of this practice, called "turnkey." So again, I was desperate, I needed business and had little money to stay alive. I had had some success in selling my metal buildings in

Louisville, a city of 900,000 population in 1968, and I advertised for a branch manager, so to speak.

I hired a guy who was in his mid-40s—Ernie Bethel. Ernie was a good salesman and together we crafted beautiful and comprehensive proposals that outshined other contractors. As there was no internet back then, it would take a Herculean effort to check us out, such as by calling Cincinnati banks or Dun & Bradstreet. It was assumed that if a firm like W. P. Butler Company had an office 100 miles from home, well, that was probably a large company. They did not know there was a "kid" on the other end of the contract.

We started landing contracts beginning in late 1968 or 1969. Over the next seven or eight years, we supplied and installed building systems or turnkey built nearly 35 buildings in Louisville and the surrounding area. We built turnkey buildings for Rohm and Haas Chemical, one 45,000-square-foot, and another 83,000-square-foot warehouse inside their plant campus. We designed and constructed two buildings for Julian P. Van Winkle of Stitzel-Weller Distillery: an automated case goods warehouse and a new 75,000-square-foot bottling plant. Mr. Van Winkle had sold his company in the course of the work on the first building to a national conglomerate that owned Tanqueray gin and Johnnie Walker scotches, and for years thereafter those products were bottled in that facility alongside Rebel Yell, and Old Fitzgerald and Old Weller bourbons. I was 29 years old when we undertook those challenges, and the contract size was near $3 million. Fifty years ago, that was a big contract.

We had proven our skill as a builder and had many photos of Louisville buildings we were responsible for as proof of our experience. No longer could anyone argue what we had built and, as a result, companies in Northern Kentucky and Cincinnati started giving us a chance, too. The local contractors with whom we would compete wondered where we came from all of a sudden, having entered our home market from a back door, so to speak.

Customers assumed that the company's presence in Louisville signaled its success, that it was a big business with enough resources to support multiple offices. That assumption certainly worked in my favor.

I think I lived more than half my time in Louisville or on the road driving back and forth. For much of that time there was not yet an interstate connecting the two cities.

Later, in the early 1970s, we undertook a challenging land development in Louisville.

On my travels in and around the metro, I noticed there was a 40-acre piece of land in a prime industrial area, and I wondered why it was undeveloped. It was the headquarters site of the then mothballed Southern Brick and Tile company. Most bricks in downtown Louisville buildings had been baked there years ago. Everyone knew the history and location of the "ole brickyard," as they affectionately labelled it. I found out that flash floods occurred in that part of Louisville and that there was a need to engineer a way to capture the water on site and pump it out to a point—an outfall ditch more than a half a mile away. No one previously had been willing to tackle the problem.

I secured the easement to do so and we embarked on the Ole Brickyard Business Park in 1973. It was very successful. We built and leased buildings, one to General Electric, and sold and built for Budweiser Distributing and other local companies. We built six speculative industrial properties and one office building on the front that we owned for 40 years. All of this was profitable and helpful to accelerate our growth.

Louisville fell on hard times following the severe recession of 1973–1974, due to it being a pilot city along with Boston for busing children to eliminate segregation. I am not sure it has ever fully regained its spirit.

We eventually closed our operations in Louisville, as we grew in other dimensions, types of properties, and locations in the Southeast, beginning in Florida.

Strategic Acts of Desperation

The company grew slowly at the start, in the late 1960s, but by 1970 we had hit $1 million in revenue. The 2022 equivalent of $1 million in 1970 is around $7.4 million, which, to me at the time was a very respectable business. But these revenues were all from selling and installing metal buildings and a few other structural roof systems sprinkled in by then. In retrospect, this particular time period was a huge turning point in our company's progress.

That year, 1970, was also the first year we started operating as a general contractor, by taking whole jobs, rather than working as a subcontractor for another general contractor firm. I hoped by that point that my track record of having designed and built buildings in the area for other companies would have carried over and given me the credentials to build on my own. That remained to be seen, even as I jumped in with both feet. We were always more than a general contractor, we were a master builder, as in the old days of Michelangelo or John Roebling. We turnkeyed the work—we designed it and we built it, both.

This was also the year we entered the business park land development business.

An even bigger problem I was having, other than establishing credibility as a builder, was finding property for my customers to build on. There were many more potential customers for my industrial buildings than there were readily available industrial lots on which to build them. General contractors in the area were happy to put up a building if you had the land ready to build on, but they weren't in the business of looking for land for them. They expected the company owners to find their own land, then choose an architect, and then a general contractor to build it. My customers wanted two, three, or four acres of land on which they could build their own buildings, but there were no such lots in the Northern Kentucky area, nor were there ready industry parks waiting for tenants.

There was industrial land farther out from center city, in Florence, Kentucky, where the local business leaders had established the Northern Kentucky Industrial Park. This not-for-profit venture consisted of thousands of acres of improved industrial land. The idea behind the industrial park had been to try to attract companies that were interested in exiting the urban center of Cincinnati due to government urban renewal programs, or other national corporations in need of additional production capacity. With acres selling there for $3,000–$4,000, as part of large parcels, the Northern Kentucky Industrial Park was very successful.

However, as I mentioned, Florence is farther out than many of my customers wanted to set up shop, and the minimum parcel size was too large for them. They wanted no more than four acres when the industrial park wanted to sell them 10 or 15.

Fortunately, I happened across an estate sale for 44 acres of undeveloped land seven miles closer to the city than Florence. The land straddled the Crescent Springs and Erlanger city limits and, although it totaled 44 acres, really only 30 would be buildable. Called the Ratterman Farm, I could purchase the land for $108,000, or $2,200 per net acre. That was for starters, before I had improved it with sewers, water, and roads, and before I had levelled the topography out. It was a very hilly, wooded property, with nearly a 70-foot vertical difference from one property line to another. It would require considerable excavating to reduce the high ground and fill in the low ground in order to prepare lots that could be sold.

But, still, I took it on. I was so excited to own a piece of land, so entrepreneurial, and it was incredibly risky for me with little financial resources. But I could see the potential even then. The land straddled two municipalities so I named it the Erlanger Crescent Springs Industrial Park.

The good news at the time was that a road had already been built along the front of the property with a big water line. It was prepped for development, in my mind. I just needed to put down $30,000 and borrow the remaining $78,000 from Covington Trust Bank.

At the purchase closing I received a $9,000 rebate related to an assessment obligation, and I saw that as a $9,000 reserve we could use to make the $1,003.80 monthly loan payments. Essentially, I had nine months to succeed, or maybe to survive is a better representation.

I was not schooled in finance. I borrowed only what I needed to get the property. I had been in business just about five years at that point, so we did have some cash flow, but it was a stretch, and upon closing I had little cash left. But I owned a piece of the "rock," wow, and not just a small piece, but 44 acres.

That was probably my first big mistake. I should have borrowed enough money to make the needed improvements on top of the land purchase. As it was, I owned the untouched land, but it needed work before I could sell any off.

The fact that I hadn't budgeted for the improvements may have added to the perception that I was a 27-year-old in over his head. I had undertaken to deliver a privately developed business park without the financial resources to finish the work. Because my plan was to sell lots for $12,500 per acre when the Northern Kentucky Industrial Park was selling acres for no more than $4,000 attracted skeptics, but theirs were larger sites, and mine were smaller but closer in to the city, yet the pricing set a new mark.

Oh, plenty of companies liked my vision, they just weren't yet convinced that I could make it happen. No one was willing to be the first company to buy in. I could get customers to water, to see my plans, but I could not yet get them to drink.

I began to panic.

The solution, as I saw it at the time, was to make progress in developing the land. I needed to clear the big trees, cut and fill the land, and build part of the roads. That way customers could begin to see the potential of the area. The only problem was that it was going to take another $40,000 to make that happen—$40,000 I definitely did not have. I attempted to borrow more, but you may recall that 1970 was a recession year and the prime interest rate was already at 8 percent. No bank would give me a second mortgage.

Knowing I had to do something, almost anything, to develop that land, I found a contractor who had fallen on hard times and who was willing to sell me his relatively new 977-H Caterpillar front-end loader for $17,000. Granted, I didn't have $17,000 either, but I went back to Covington Trust, hoping that the fact that the machinery could be used as collateral might sway them.

Now, at the time, Covington Trust was a very small bank. Its owners—John Krumpelman, Don Conrad, and Robert "R.C." Durr—were all entrepreneurs, and David Herriman, a smart younger guy, was the president. I was lucky to have R.C. Durr, the largest road contractor in the area, on the executive committee, because he likely understood my challenge. And as it turned out just maybe he wanted to help out a young entrepreneur. I never knew, but the bank did agree to loan me the money I needed for the Caterpillar on a chattel lien program where if I missed a payment, the equipment would be seized. That worked for me.

I immediately got to work. I hired a skilled operator named Ron Foltz, who was just as hard a worker as I was, and together we made it happen. Ron ran the dozer all day and I'd come down after work and run it until it got dark. I was a capable operator as well. We traded off on the weekends, working that dozer seven days a week.

We took down trees, moved dirt from one end of the property to the other, filled in the low areas, and cut the path for the streets. In a matter of weeks, the land started to resemble a real deal, and the buyers were convinced. They saw progress and they believed, signed on the dotted line.

It was a lesson in marketing 101—that is, "in order for anyone to commit, they must first believe." They had to see my vision and believe it was going to happen. I often mused that I could have been moving the dirt from one end to the other and then picking it up and putting it back, it didn't matter.

My approach was one-stop shopping. Companies could choose the lot they wanted to build on within the acreage, and then I would design and build their vision in one fell swoop. Two sales in one—land and construction. Combining all of those services under one roof introduced me to a new concept, and that led us into the land-development business going forward.

A Hard Lesson in Property Titles

Of course, nothing is ever that simple, and this deal was a case-in-point. The Erlanger land was being sold as part of an estate, which had been left to Mr. Ratterman's widow. The property was part of his estate, which was to be transferred to her on his death. The transfer should have been a matter of paperwork, really. However, likely in the hopes of clarifying or driving home the point, Mr. Ratterman then made the mistake of writing his own will. In it he stated:

> "I give and bequeath to my beloved wife Bernadine, all that I have and possess . . ."

and if he had stopped there, we would have been fine. However, he continued:

> "... for her to use and enjoy for the rest of her natural life. I also empower her as my executor to dispose of it as she sees fit, if necessary, without hindrance."

That specific terminology then threw the whole estate into question and, much to my dismay, paused the deal. My attorneys had inspected the title in customary ways before I closed on the property and had sanctioned it. I had even bought title insurance as part of the initial purchase of the 44 acres, but I hadn't realized that as I began subdividing it, my customers would then also buy title insurance after me. And that's when the questions arose.

After I had bought the property and started selling off pieces to build on, the attorneys involved in those transaction questioned whether Mr. Ratterman had meant that his widow should be able to enjoy the property as long as she was alive, which could be interpreted as a "life estate." And in that case, he wasn't actually bequeathing "fee simple" ownership. Mr. Ratterman also added to his bequest that "I empower her to dispose of it as she sees fit," which would suggest fee simple ownership except that he added "if necessary."

While the lawyers discussed how to interpret the will, my future in business was increasingly in question once again. If, in the end, the title couldn't be cleared, I couldn't sell any of the land I had just bought, despite owing a growing $78,000 obligation. I was working against a clock.

I had put everything I owned, including my future prospects, on the line for this deal. As it turns out, this first real estate venture is only one of multiple times I bet the farm. The longer the legal discussions continued, the greater my fears grew that I would not be able to make my plans for an industrial park a reality.

My reasoning for acquiring this land had merit. There was for sure a demand for my sites. But for each contract I entered to sell a parcel, there would be a different attorney to close the sale, a different title insurance company to deal with, and different opinions on the intent of the will. At one point, in 1971, this issue became extremely acute as I sought and successfully received the nod from Puritan Chemical Company to sell them a site and to build a building for them. However, that contract had its own complexities to deal with: I had to agree to deliver the warehouse portion of the building in only eight weeks, including design and site preparation and the remainder, including offices, four weeks later. Puritan was closing an operation in Detroit and relocating because of union troubles. They were under the gun, which meant that I, too, was being rushed.

Pioneer Title Company, a large insurance company, hired a local attorney to do the title search for Puritan Chemical, and that attorney raised a red flag when he did his title search. He said the title was definitely clouded by the language of the will. My heart dropped. I was stretched thin financially, and the deal meant everything for the company. I couldn't afford any kind of delay.

After some time when the efforts to convince him that the title was clean, my attorneys who had done the title work for me when I bought the land scheduled a phone meeting directly with Pioneer Title to argue how they interpreted Mr. Ratterman's intent. They worked to persuade the title company attorneys to believe their conclusions, rather than the opinion of the outside attorney. Anyone who knows real estate and title understands that this would likely be an impossible task. All of my work to get this contract was on the table, and maybe the entire company, because if this company rejected the title, so would others. I was kicking myself for not being smarter. I had thought that once I had title insurance, that would take care of any questions, but it did not protect the buyers who would come behind me in ownership. I was stuck, with no apparent solution other than for my attorneys to prevail, which was unlikely, I knew. The reality of the situation hit me hard.

For the first time in my career, I closed the door to my office, which was then in a rented space associated with a hotel outside of Covington, closed my eyes, and prayed. I remember exactly what I prayed:

> "Not as a bribe, but in recognition of Your presence in my life,
> God, I will quit smoking immediately."

I wasn't bartering, but, rather, offering, in faith, a sign of my acceptance of God's will, and a reaffirmation of my commitment to Him. I quit smoking at that very moment, accepting whatever outcome was in store for me. I continued to sit in my office, awaiting some kind of news from my attorneys.

Maybe an hour and a half later, the phone rang. To my surprise and immense relief, the title company had done a flip-flop and decided they would insure the title for Puritan. I unlocked and opened my office door. The deal was moving forward. We had to remove more than 20 feet of earth overburden from the site and build an entire building in eight weeks.

I had a commitment from American Buildings Company that they would engineer, fabricate, and deliver the pre-engineered steel building package in just two weeks. We had to install foundations and utilities, in addition to the mass grading, which we did just in time for the steel. We met the agreed-upon terms and 90 days became the standard for our company to perform from that time forward.

Was my decision to quit smoking a bribe? I don't know. I didn't mean it as such, only as a sign that my faith was in God and that whatever His will, I would accept it. Well, my prayer was answered and my faith again reinforced. That, too, has happened many times over in my career. I was only 28 at the time, but had smoked since age 16 (a lot, they tell me). I quit for the next nine years, gained, at one point, 67 pounds, and after picking up a cigar at a golf outing, the addiction to cigarettes was back in full force. I smoked again for seven and a half years, lost most of the weight gain, and then quit for good.

Looking back over many years, it is clear that acquiring that land and developing that business park was indeed pivotal. Taking on our first turnkey design-and-construction contract that same year, 1970, while simultaneously entering the real estate developing arena, together was a giant step in shaping the enterprise W. P. Butler Company was destined to become. We signed multiple sales contracts for land sites, as well as contracts to build buildings in relatively short order, both here and in Louisville. The Erlanger Crescent Springs Park was exactly that—a spring forward—and put us into a second business only five years from our founding, that of commercial real estate development

It was an education for me, a lesson learned. In the process of working with me to buy the site for a prospective customer's new corporate home, the selection of my company to design and construct was almost automatic. It was in getting comfortable with me while choosing a site, they felt comfortable with our ability to deliver a quality building product as well. That first land development was a big growth step. At one point we had five buildings under construction simultaneously in the park. The W. P. Butler Company had truly transitioned from a metal building supplier and erector to a full design-build-construct contractor and developer of business parks. One of the first turning points indeed.

This, the first industrial park development, was quickly followed by two more, one in Blue Ash in suburban Cincinnati and the other previously mentioned Ole Brickyard Business Park in Louisville.

Being on the Leading Edge Provides an Edge on Competition

Soon after the first land development, in 1972, we built our first speculative multi-tenant industrial building in Blue Ash within our second business park, called Acres for Industry. Building speculative buildings was considered extraordinarily risky, rare in conservative Cincinnati, but it was already being done in some parts of the country. We were invited to a meeting of industrial developers that was held in Cleveland. The National Association of Industrial Parks (NAIP) was in its infancy. The developers met to share their experiences with building buildings in advance of having a customer, and then leasing them as a novel way to get business where the user did not want to spend the time or trouble of building. Our strategy was to build a building that could meet a wide range of uses, one that one or more tenants could lease, and for short term commitments. It was not only considered novel, but highly speculative and risk-prone. But because the developer members of NAIP shared openly, we learned how to avoid mistakes, what size to build, how to design and how to market our buildings. Speculative building, like design-build turnkey services, eventually became commonplace, but again we were on the leading edge, and that made a difference in our trajectory.

Building buildings for the market quickly became a way of life. We developed more than 8 million square feet, maybe even 10 million, in the 35 years that followed in various cities. We developed buildings that we owned, leased, managed, and held long-term. However, periodically we would sell one to generate more capital for growth. We discontinued building industrial buildings maybe 20 years ago in favor of office buildings, hotels, and other mixed-use investments that would provide a bigger return of value relative to the effort involved in building, leasing, and managing properties.

Over the years I have often referred to the three separate measures of return: return on investment, return on equity, and return on effort. The last item is difficult to measure but, in my mind, has always been equally important if not more important than the first two. Our time, our personal time is maybe the most expensive commodity we employ. Emphasis on the added measure "return on effort" has potentially been one of the more effective tools in our management toolbox. After all, the people are the key to the outcome. The practice has helped to seek and retain highly productive managers, and to be able to compensate advantageously as a result. Our focus on productivity has often led us to replace two positions with only one individual of a broader capability, and with more hands-on tendencies. With fewer people to rely upon, fewer people to manage, the opportunity to reward the star producers is greatly enhanced—and when a downcycle occurs, the enterprise is able to avoid layoffs that otherwise may be required. It is not a management concept one often reads about.

Chapter 6

Black Markets and White Knights

Throughout the early days of the company, I invested substantially all of our earnings right back into the business, to fuel more growth. That, too, became a truism throughout the years, but I always steered clear of investing in what I considered the truly risky investments, such as oil, coal, or horses—Kentucky things! The outsized risks in speculative development of empty buildings were enough to satisfy my appetite in that regard. Despite this, oil had a major impact on our small company in the early 1970s.

Efforts by the Organization of the Petroleum Exporting Countries (OPEC) in 1973 to raise prices and to punish America for certain political differences, gave rise to a boycott, where oil production was cut off, driving the price of gasoline through the roof—and making it incredibly scarce. But the damage went far beyond the two-block-long lines to the gas pumps. Because many construction products, including roofing for industrial buildings, and asphalt for paving parking lots are oil-based, we saw prices for those raw materials quickly skyrocket. The price of steel also climbed. Every week it would increase, with prices only locked in with a non-cancellable order; otherwise, prices could not be guaranteed for more than five days, that's how quickly the numbers were rising. But even if we did have a firm contract, that did not mean that we would receive its fulfillment. Our roofing and paving contractors defaulted on their contracts because the costs of materials increased relentlessly, and we had to pay another contractor much more to complete the work.

In addition, diesel fuel was just a difficult as gasoline to get and I had those big guzzling bulldozers, and earth haulers, and trucks to operate. In addition to constructing buildings and developing our own lands, we had also taken on contracts to move earth for other developers as well. But it was impossible to get the fuel, almost at any price. A so-called black market evolved and one identified supplier found a way, but I had to buy the fuel in bulk—and in cash. So, in crisis mode, I acquired a parcel of industrial land in Erlanger one mile from the office, fenced it, excavated and buried four large fuel storage tanks that would hold 40,000 gallons of fuel—that is a lot of fuel. I had to buy a used fuel truck as well to deliver to our jobs. But it became even more complicated, in order to secure the fuel, I remember meeting the owner of the wholesale provider at 3 a.m., the middle of the night, opening the yard, and handing him a check on the spot for a load of fuel on more than one occasion. I cannot think of an example that would better illustrate the acute nature of this period in time and the sharp recession that occurred, and to what extremes we had to engage, and the stresses we had to endure in order to survive . . . .

This had followed a period of high growth for our emerging enterprise, from revenues of $1 million in 1970 to annual construction revenues of $7.5 million in 1974—that is 7.5 times growth in four years. This was a major milestone for Corporex, which I took as a sign that we were doing well, that we were here to stay. Of course, the oil embargo then quickly created a situation of panic. It was like walking off a cliff. In the next year, 1975, our revenues dropped to $1.7 million. At that point, we were completing the contracts we had on the books, but nothing more.

Perhaps more concerning was the fact that there were no construction contracts to be had; new building was effectively halted. The world had stopped, it seemed. Building projects were actually cancelled, terminated by their owners in the middle of construction, and projects we had been near securing contracts for were shelved completely and permanently. I recall three separate significant contracts that were imminent: two buildings for the building supply company Lowe's and a large supermarket for Kroger near the University of Cincinnati. I was able to value engineer, or redesign, the foundations in order to get the project into Kroger's budget, but the project did not move forward due to the recession, and ironically after that, we never ever built for Kroger or for Lowe's. We just moved on with other contracts after the recession.

The impacts of this oil embargo recession were extreme and the scramble to save the company incredible. Going into this collapse in 1974–75, we had a field construction payroll of 181 tradesmen, an office staff of 38, consisting of architects, engineers, construction pros, accounting employees, and salespeople. We had eight steel erection crews, concrete construction crews, and had amassed nearly 25 pieces of big earth-moving equipment, dozers, heavy earth scrapers, cranes, and a big Mack tractor to move the equipment around.

This recession was best described as a reversal—all back full. Everything came to a screeching halt.

We ran out of work completely. Nearly all the operations wound down. It was an incredible lesson in economics that, being only 30 years old, I, frankly, was not ready for.

The entire profit we had accumulated since the company's founding nine years earlier was lost in only one year, in 1975. At one point, our balance sheet indicated approximately $100,000 in receivables and $800,000 in owed payables. We were essentially broke, once again.

We laid off all but two of the field people as the projects were completed. Imagine, from 181 tradesmen to only 2. One of the two people we kept was our key site and field manager, a fellow named Howard Neltner. I do not remember the other. We reduced the office staff to 11, and I personally did not take a salary or draw of any kind for the next two years.

Because of the spike in oil prices and shortages, the price of coal down in Kentucky skyrocketed, driving up demand. Many people asked me to take the equipment down to the mountains in Kentucky to strip mine. That to me was dangerous. But heavy equipment like we had was in big demand for mining, so we sold the dozers and loaders, and scrapers, too, for use in coal mining to get some cash, and we begged and borrowed wherever we could in order to make payroll with what was left. But we also remained determined, having faith that one day things would turn around—and failure was not acceptable.

Selling the equipment was opportunistic, entrepreneurial, and a smart move, though I don't think we knew just how smart at the time. We have never again acquired earth-moving equipment. In those days, the tradition was to provide employees with leased vehicles. After laying off all those people, there were 22 such cars in our office lot on which I was making the payments. Going forward, we provided car allowances. When an employee left the company, so did the car.

We undoubtedly hurt subcontractors because we could not pay, not on time, and, to this day, I regret that. However, over the next four years, as we regained our footing, we paid everyone in full, with whatever profit we could extract through continuing sales of properties, new construction contracts, and anywhere else we found we could get cash. We have never had bank lines of credit to draw on like larger firms. We have always financed all operations out of our resources, using no lines of credit. We do borrow heavily on projects where mortgage financing will permit, but never again did we have a significant mortgage on land holdings.

Notwithstanding the stresses of the time, we were moving forward and making progress. Armed with all the pictures, the evidence of buildings we had built in Louisville, and by owning the land, which gave us credibility, we were successfully garnering some contracts to build within all of our parks.

Union Trouble

We encountered our first problem with unions around this time, in the mid-1970s, while building a 15,000-square-foot building for a customer named Kent Manufacturing. Kent Manufacturing had to have its building built within 90 days because Kent had agreed to sell its existing, larger manufacturing property on the condition that they could convey within that tight time period. I seem to recall that the company had suffered, as most companies had, greatly during the recession of the time and would only be saved by selling its factory building. The company's survival required a new smaller home quickly, 90 days total.

I had only recently built a building for Puritan Chemical in the park and knew it could be done, so I committed again.

Things were going well. We had the steel up in the air, the metal roof and walls in place, and were in the process of pouring the concrete floor when the building trade unions decided to strike. They threw up a picket line and stopped the concrete truck drivers, who were unionized, from entering our work site. Their timing was intentional of course, to catch us in the middle of a half-completed section of the pour with fresh concrete. What to do?

Without thinking a lot, I called the concrete supplier and asked them to allow me to drive the trucks that were lined up along the roadway waiting for direction. The only thing worse than an incomplete concrete slab is concrete curing and hardening inside the truck itself. Someone said "Okay," the drivers got out of their cabs, I got in, put the trucks in reverse with the backup beepers sounding, and began going backwards into the project site. The picketers stepped aside and we finished the pour.

We had just finished when all hell broke loose for the concrete suppliers. The union bosses had reached the owners to warn them not to comply with my request, but it was too late. We got the job done and moved Kent in within the 90-day agreement. We also experienced a similar picket line on the Lookout Corporate Center project when we brought in a steel erection contractor out of Tennessee. But I met with the union representatives, we bargained that I would award a portion of the trades to union contractors and continue to operate "open shop"—in other words, with a mixed unionized/non-unionized tradesmen methodology. Generally, we were able to do that and to maintain a candid and equitable relationships with the unions for our projects. Eventually this practice, too, has become more commonplace in most cities in the United States.

U.S. Steel to the Rescue

One project that was a huge contributor to our recovery following the OPEC recession in the mid-1970s, and which allowed us to pay our many past-due debts, was for U.S. Steel Supply Corporation. Ironically, in 1974 or 1975, U.S. Steel very politely turned us down when we expressed interest in bidding on the company's new distribution center in Cincinnati. Executives said, "Mr. Butler, you have a fine company, but you are just not big enough to work for U.S. Steel." I recall being pleased with his straightforward statement at the time. I think it was taken as a challenge to grow.

U.S. Steel took bids for the project and the quoted costs significantly exceeded their budget, so they did not award the work then. This period was one of high inflationary growth—materials and labor were skyrocketing. I happened to be in Chicago two years later in 1976 and cold-called the top guy at the headquarters of the supply division to discuss the status of that building. He was an executive vice president, and we had a nice chat about the project, and I told him I could design and build that building within their budget using my methods and energy.

Their plan was to consolidate two distribution centers—one currently in Louisville and one in Cincinnati—into one larger facility. I asked him about the net cost to add this new facility after selling the other two. In other words, by selling those older warehouses and using those funds to help pay for the new building, it would help him to get the new center. "We do not get a credit for turning in buildings under the policy of the company," he told me. So I came up with a novel idea: I offered to take those two buildings in trade and charge him only for the difference. That got his attention. Soon I was talking again to my friend in Pittsburgh who had turned me down previously. I learned that U.S. Steel had never done a 1031 tax-free exchange under IRS rules. To them, this was quite novel indeed, and I suspect it was for many companies.

I had no idea how I would make it happen financially, but I was determined to figure it out. After all, my company was limping along. We negotiated intensely, wrote a complex agreement, and I set out to get the money to finance three buildings—one in Louisville, one in the Cincinnati urban area, and the new

80,000-sqare-foot, 70-foot-tall heavy-duty warehouse. I had to secure sufficient money to acquire the land, fund the entire new construction without U.S. Steel paying me a dime, and then fund the money to buy the two empty warehouses after we traded U.S. Steel the new building for the two older buildings.

My attorney, Jerry Teller, arranged a meeting with a gentleman named Jim Markley at Provident Bank. I had never done business with Provident, but I had prepared a professional presentation that got his attention. In the middle of the meeting, Joe Rippe Sr., the bank president, came by. He asked me four key questions and then concluded: "Hmm, you have a chance to make $400,000 with this deal, is that so?" "Yessir," I responded. He then said, "I want 4 points, and 4 over." This means I would have to pay him 4 percent times the loan amount up front just to make the loan to me, and then a 4 percent interest rate premium over the top of what was then called bank prime rate. That is a lot. I needed this loan in the worst way, but I responded, "I have 2 points and 2 over prime in my plan." He retorted, "3 points and 3 over. Now I have to go." And he left. I looked across the table and asked Markley, "Do I understand this correctly? Did we just make a deal?" He nodded.

That was in 1977. We caught the inflationary spiral on construction costs on the downside following the recession, purchased the materials and subcontracts for a big savings on the new construction, and the margin on the project doubled to about $350,000. We sold the Louisville building for a profit of $40,000 before we had to take title from U.S. Steel, and we leased the Cincinnati warehouse for three years on a lease-purchase deal, and then sold it to the tenant. In all we made $750,000 over a three to four-year period, and that allowed us to pay our past-due accounts and to get back on our feet financially.

A Shift in Business Practices

What we took away from these trying years was to never again hire our own field personnel. From 1975 on, we became construction managers using specialty contractors to perform carpentry, concrete, steel erection—the kind of work we did with our own people and equipment before the recession. We have continued to use this method even today. Relatively new in methodology then, it is now pretty universal among builders. We organized and managed many specialty subcontractors rather than direct employees. We never bought big earth moving equipment again and we substituted car allowances for leased vehicles for our employees. This was another turning point—a new way to do business, but smarter. The idea was to prioritize one's focus on managing results over managing people, so to speak. This principle can be applied in any business type or activity.

While the U.S. Steel project helped us pay our past-due obligations, it did not restore any substance to the balance sheet to overcome the losses. I did another very unusual maneuver in this same period that made all the difference. Again, because of the severe recession, there were other investors on the rocks. Actually, I did the same bold move two times, when I bought two parcels of land from two separate owners where the values of the property far exceeded the outstanding mortgage and the actual lender on the properties would lend me more than the actual cost of the transaction. In one case, I bought land from Stan Grueninger, next to his Oldsmobile distributorship in Woodlawn, Cincinnati. I paid him $300,000, but his lender agreed to give me a loan of $450,000. I closed the deal and put $150,000 cash in the top of my balance sheet. In the other case I bought from a group of investors led by John Krumpelman in Edgewood, Kentucky, an 8-acre parcel that I quickly developed into a retail and office complex called Heritage International. I recall borrowing once again an excess $150,000 from his friendly bank. Together I had added approximately $700,000 in mortgage liability, but also $300,000 to my balance sheet—and that cash-on-hand gave me a new credibility.

We spent the next five years, 1976 through 1980, rebuilding the company. Fortunately, we bounced back relatively quickly to reach annual revenues ranging from $9 million to $10 million for 1976, 1977, 1978, 1979, and by the close of year 1980, we had $16 million in revenues and $1 million in free and clear cash-on-hand in the bank. I finally had learned a new four-letter word: C-A-S-H. Never again did I want to be in such dire straits, but another economic lesson was soon at hand.

But the late 1970s despite the difficulties were robust growth years for us, and a combination of actions helped us build our coffers; periods like this make one learn hard lessons, or is it lesson, the hard way. Either way, in retrospect it appears that bath by fire enabled me, and had something to do with what was about to happen in the next decade when we grew many times over and in multiple dimensions, especially geography.

CirclePort—at Cincinnati's Front Door

One project at the core of our rebuilding, which began in the late 1970s and stretched into the 1980s and beyond is the CirclePort Business Park, near the Greater Cincinnati/Northern Kentucky International Airport. The main airport for Cincinnati is actually located in Kentucky, along I-275. Understanding the importance of this air transportation hub, we purchased an 80-acre parcel of land along a road near the airport called Mineola Pike. At the time, however, there was no direct access to I-275 from Mineola Pike, so it was not the easiest to get to. The land at that time was mostly farms, still owned by various families.

As part of the Governor's Economic Development Task Force in 1981, the construction of the access road had been designated as one of the key locations where the state of Kentucky could help the Northern Kentucky community. We knew there would be great attention paid to this area. Then, in the 1980s, we purchased an adjacent 200-acre farm, plus three other parcels over time, to form a 660-acre plot where I foresaw a premier mixed-use business park at the front door to the city. To share our vision, we developed master plans and pictures of what could be, to introduce what we believed could be a quality business park filled with corporate headquarters and smaller industrial users, to form a mixed-used development powered by the latest technology.

The connection to I-275 didn't occur until 1987, 10 years later, which did slow down development of the business park.

Cincinnati residents and business leadership may never realize what a favor we did them by sticking to our original vision for CirclePort, indeed from 40 years ago. We wanted to present a positive image of the community to those arriving to our community by plane. To me, the international airport is Greater Cincinnati's front door to the world. That was important to me, as a proud native of the area, but it was also in keeping with our corporate commitment to making long-term contributions to our community, which has always been part of our mission. Some investors and builders feel that land available for development is intended for the purpose of making money, without regard to its long-term impact. Their goal is to make as many sales as possible as quickly as possible in order to maximize profit. I have always believed that in some ways, we are stewards of the land, and that as such, we have a responsibility to develop it in a responsible way, with an eye to the impact on the surrounding communities. In the case of CirclePort, sites like this close to the airport were somewhat scarce; we could have sold it quickly for pure industrial uses. We could have lined Interstate 275 with big buildings, non-descript boxes, so to speak, that travelers would see as they drove toward downtown from the airport. Industrial distribution is what the marketplace supported for many, many years. Instead, we held firm to our vision for CirclePort Park as an attractive front door, developing it slowly and with much architectural determination, with office buildings, research, and hotels on the frontage, recognizable names.

Ultimately, over the course of 30 years we attracted a bevy of corporate names residents could be proud of. We lured Citicorp to locate a credit card collection office in one of the speculative office buildings. We designed and built a beautiful building for a technology unit of Cincinnati Bell—a training center for Japanese telephone companies, for which they had entered a huge contract to provide software. This later was doubled in size when it became the manufacturing support headquarters for Toyota USA. We built an office building speculatively in which General Electric located its IT subsidiary enterprise. We designed and built the U.S. headquarters campus for a German firm named Wild Flavors, a beautiful facility. We constructed multiple multi-tenant office buildings and attracted many regional headquarters to the park. We also built multiple service-center-type buildings and leased and sold some to Equitable Life. It is a business park everyone can be proud of, and provides an attractive entranceway to the entire Cincinnati and Northern Kentucky population center.

The airport and the highway through our CirclePort development remains the gateway to the world for our cities. Nice-looking office buildings with reflective glass and big names on them, painted a better picture of welcome than cold industrial warehouse boxes. While some in real estate would have concluded that we simply did not market well, we were actually pioneering once again to ensure that our development made a big and long-term difference to the perception we wanted to create of a quality and progressive community. We tried to do our part to make a lasting contribution to the landscape and the prosperity of our area, which was the purpose of Corporex from the start—to leave the area better than we found it.

Today, there are still 200 acres of fully developed and debt-free land in the park waiting for the next stage of development there. The recent construction of a $4 billion Amazon global logistics facility on the airport grounds between the runways has shined a spotlight on the area again. From its location at the airport, Amazon will sort and ship packages, through its Prime Air enterprise, internationally to Europe and Latin America non-stop, and to Asia after a West Coast stop. In light of this important tenant, Corporex is re-evaluating the type of buildings it should develop, in order to accommodate the vendors and consultants that will be necessary to serve this massive facility.

The Lookout Corporate Center

The Lookout House was a popular night club in Northern Kentucky featuring fine dining, dancing, big bands, and expensive celebrity shows. It was called the Lookout House because it was located on one of the highest points of land and had been the location of a lookout post to the South during the Civil War. Kentucky was neutral during the war, at least near Cincinnati in the north. But the Union army set up military camps on the high grounds where they could look to the

South advantageously. Our cities became known as Fort Wright, Fort Mitchell, and Fort Thomas for the high-ranking commanders, General Thomas, General Wright, and General Mitchell, all Northern names.

The nightclub was named the Lookout House and a man named Dick Schilling sold it to a group of investors from Ohio in the early 1970s who then ruined the business. It mysteriously burned to the ground in 1973, and a year or so later came to my attention. We negotiated a simple option agreement to acquire the site for $450,000. We secured the financing from a local bank and the seller was required to deliver a clear title.

I was about to get yet another lesson in real estate mistakes.

I needed a clear title on the property because I had drawn plans for a big hotel and conference center that Sheraton Hotels was interested in and which a life insurance company was ready to finance. But the seller could not deliver title because Mr. Schilling had acquired a sliver of land from the neighboring drive-in theatre many years before and attached it to the larger Lookout House plot. National Amusements in Boston owned the drive-in theatre, and it was they who would have to resolve title with the sellers.

When Dick Schilling had acquired the land, it was for added parking. So, at the time, he agreed to a title restriction that read: *"Nothing shall be built on this property which would cause any glare, sheen, shine, ray, or light, in the direction of the drive-in theatre."* The drive-in owners wanted to be sure there would be no interference with their ability to show movies at night. Imagine that: "no sheen in the direction of" the neighboring property. It was an almost impossible requirement for any other use; the sellers did not know their own property.

The seller had earlier filed bankruptcy and the court appointed a former Kroger executive as the trustee of the assets. John Lockhart arranged a meeting with the owner of National Amusements in Boston—none other than the infamous multibillionaire Sumner Redstone. Redstone's company, National Amusements, now owned the drive-in theatre. John and his 32-year-old developer, me, flew to Boston for the meeting. We waited an hour for Mr. Redstone and were finally escorted into a boardroom with a lengthy table. Mr. Redstone sat at the far end. We put our stack of plans on the table, and John asked Sumner to have the plans reviewed for our hotel and to sign off that this was okay to construct next to his drive-in theatre.

The meeting was short, as Sumner Redstone raised his head up only slightly to look in the direction of my complete set of blueprints, and said, "There are not possibly enough drawings for me to ever come to a decision." Then he left the room. John and I were dumbfounded. We went back to the airport with plans rolled under my arms and boarded a Delta flight to Cincinnati.

Sometime thereafter, we negotiated to acquire the site from the seller at a discount, for $300,000, and went about building a smaller office building that continued to use the sliver of land for only a surface parking lot. Lookout Corporate Center, Northern Kentucky's first high-rise, was the beginning of our foray into high-rise office buildings. We opened its doors in 1981 and moved our headquarters to that location for the next 10 years.

When I read in later years how Mr. Redstone had acquired Blockbuster Video for $300 million and then Blockbuster went bankrupt, essentially, well, I would be reminded of his cold-hearted treatment of us, and I must admit that I did not empathize with Redstone's big loss.

Everyone Needs Someone to Report To

Corporex has had a board of directors since 1977, because I have always believed that everyone needs someone to report to, including the company owner. I also believed that surrounding oneself with smart people was almost guaranteed to yield success; I knew I would benefit from the counsel of more experienced executives. It is amazing how a small company can attract high-caliber executives to help a young aspiring businessperson like me at that time. Somewhat in turn, I understand why at this point in life one of my most enjoyable activities is to work with young people as a mentor, and work with CEOs of the charitable organizations I chair and their affiliated entities.

Fortunately for us, we landed top talent for the board through the years, starting with George Scheper, whom I had met at a wedding reception and got to know in a social setting. George was the chief financial officer at DuBois Chemicals, a big company in Cincinnati, at the time, and went on to become CEO. After a few lunches, George agreed to become the first member of the Corporex board of directors.

With George on board, we then added a very senior person from Massachusetts Mutual Life Insurance (MassMutual), Ed Kulik, who was a real estate executive there. It was Ed who suggested we take a look at Tampa for our first outreach office. Others who also joined the board included my brother-in-law John Klare and Jerry Teller, who was our general counsel. Later, in the 1980s, we added a gentleman named Don Clark, who was president of an identical construction development company owned by McCormick Tea and Spice in Baltimore. Our firms did not compete directly, so Don was free to participate, and did until 1991 or 1992, when I disbanded the board because I was concerned about the potential exposure of the board members to liability during the credit crunch, which was a threat once again to our existence, our very survival. We did not have directors' insurance either, nor could we afford it. I did reconstitute the board later, with new people, except for Jerry Teller, and it remains a vibrant force in our corporate structure.

Chapter 7

"First We Make Sure We're Right, Then We Show Them Speed"

I spent the period from 1976 to 1980 building a balance sheet. I learned a big lesson from the pain of the recession—that I needed to have a greater amount of cash, a stronger balance sheet in order to withstand such downturns in the economy. We held growth in check, focused instead on profit, and built up cash in the checking accounts. For four years we held sales flat, to $9 million, on average, did not hire, and just worked on delivering the bottom line and saving money. The entire 1970s had been our first exposure to runaway inflation. Material and labor costs continued to escalate at an incredible rate, unsustainably as it turned out.

Inflation hit 12 percent by 1979, topping out at just over 13 percent, and the Federal Reserve chairman was then replaced to try to stop the stampede. Arthur Burns was out and Paul Volcker was in. Volcker's solution was to turn off the spigot of new money flow into the economy, immediately, starve it. The result? The economy came to a screeching halt. Short-term interest rates rose to unprecedented territory, at around 20 percent, and unemployment followed suit, rising to nearly 11 percent in 1981.

Volcker put a halt to inflation and gradually, over a number of years, interest rates receded, as the Fed increased money supply. The next challenge, of course, was restarting the economy. I had begun to study money supply after the oil embargo induced a recession and had a sense of what this meant. What followed were seven to nine years of explosive growth in real estate, and for Corporex too.

While Volcker was working on how to bring down interest rates while curbing inflation, I was working on how to level out corporate revenues. Building industrial buildings in Cincinnati and Kentucky required moving earth, creating level places for the big industrial buildings we were constructing. To cut hillsides and fill in the earth to level sites could only be done during the four to six months of dry weather during the year. Consequently, while we could expedite building for six months, we had to carry our overhead of employees through the winter, which cost us most of the profit we had generated. This cycle occurred repeatedly, which was a serious problem.

My solution was to establish a presence in the nation's Deep South, where the climate was more temperate and we could build year-round, or, alternatively, to begin building multistory buildings here at home, where workers would be able to get back to work quickly after it rained, and which did not require large cuts and fills like industrial buildings do.

We actually did both. In 1980, I had researched Houston, Dallas, and Tampa as potential new markets. We went with Tampa, because it was evolving commercially at the time and there were fewer real estate developers with whom we would be competing.

Era of Explosive Growth and Challenges

We opened an office in Tampa in 1981, at the same time as we began work on the Lookout Corporate Center, a nine-story office building on top of the hill in Fort Wright, Kentucky. The Lookout building was the first multistory structure of its kind since John R. Coppin built his building at Seventh and Madison Avenue 50 or 60 years earlier. That building is now Hotel Covington, a very successful redevelopment project.

But, at the time, our new nine-story building was the energy of the conversation at the Christmas parties that year. It was a lesson to me at the time to observe how one building could create excitement in the entire community. I came to realize how buildings and quality developments can move a community and its citizens forward.

In Florida, we undertook development of more office buildings and industrial buildings, all on speculation, without tenants committed in advance. In hindsight, money was unusually available to even a small company like Corporex at the time, to build speculative office and industrial buildings where there was not a user identified. Such speculative lending on the part of the banking industry in America would have a day of reckoning for all of us, both lenders and borrowers, later in the decade. We also built buildings for others, including of all things a giant blimp hangar for Goodyear at the Pompano, Florida, airport. That building was a feat, as it was a 160 feet clear span and 160 feet tall too—large enough to hold two blimps. Although we ended up losing money building it, it remains a source of pride for the company to have been involved in its construction. We never backed away from challenging tasks. But we did get a marketing benefit from it when we developed a full-page ad with our name on the side of a blimp and the inscription: "maybe we should buy a blimp."

In Tampa we acquired a 62-acre site for a business park, and also a tract of land on the other side of Tampa next to the airport on which we built three office buildings called Presidents Plaza. Eventually the 62-acre site on the east side grew to a 100-acre development. In Corporex Business Park, we quickly sold a large parcel to Citicorp for a processing center, and built a number of speculative multi-tenant single-story business centers and a few office buildings. Tampa and the entire South and Southeast markets were experiencing a huge boost, and we got boosted along as well. Lenders were willing to provide abundant funding because there was so much growth and migration occurring in the sunbelt. It accelerated our growth in not only revenues but also in stature and perception as an office building developer in addition to industrial classes.

The World Grows Smaller

The year 1981 was also the year that the company bought its first airplane. I've often said that "airplanes made our company," because in almost the same time as you could drive to Columbus or Louisville, you could fly to Tampa, a more robust growth location.

It's a fair question to ask why a small company with revenues of approximately $25 million, mostly construction in nature, would even entertain the idea of buying a brand new $2 million airplane; $2,175,000 was actually the listed price for the model we chose. Little did I know that very few people like myself ever purchased a new-from-the-factory plane; most purchased a used one because only large corporations could afford such investments. In fact, we have since stepped up four separate times to larger, faster aircraft, all pre-owned by large firms.

My motivation had been tied to a project, a tax problem. We had constructed a major industrial project called the Florence Space Center in a joint venture with New York Life, and we were anticipating a substantial profit on the construction. But we could not access the cash, and we would need whatever cash we could access to serve our share of the carrying costs of these two speculative industrial buildings containing 450,000 square feet. So I was looking at a potentially large tax bill, without the cash resources.

But in 1980, Ronald Reagan was elected president of the United States. Recall that in 1980, interest rates were at their peak—near 20 percent. On the surface, that would be enough to scare off a buyer. In fact, it did. No one was buying airplanes. No one. But Reagan had just passed the Accelerated Cost Recovery Act (ACRA) legislation to stimulate the country out of recession. That was 1981, the same year I opened our first outlying office in Tampa, 1,000 miles away. According to the ACRA, if a person bought a new airplane, that person could get tax credits against his tax obligations, and other tax-advantaged benefits. I was scurrying to find a way to offset those taxes we were facing.

At the time, board member George Scheper, shared that DuBois had two airplanes. George was a proponent of private airplanes in general, especially because he was a family man, and he said that by having an airplane I could get home to be with family more often. So I found a Procter & Gamble pilot who acted as my consultant. He told me that, "There is only one correct plane to buy—the very popular corporate King Air 200, a high-end turbine prop-jet."

The dealer he recommended was Aviation Sales in Dayton. To make a long story short, Aviation Sales brought down a plane one Saturday morning and I took a ride. The salesman asked me if I liked it, and, of course, who wouldn't?! But the price, what was I getting into, I wanted to know. The listed price, he told me, was $2,175,000.

My consulting pilot had warned me that "they never discount a King Air." And did I really need it? Of course not, not by any logical criteria. And I was scared—but me being me, I made him an offer. I offered to give him a deposit of $25,000 and sign a contract for $1,700,000, which would have been a substantial discount. In making the offer, I embarrassed Ken Weber, my consultant. The salesman got angry, actually indignant, and scolded me with a raised voice. That was my opportunity to let it go, to walk out. But no, not me. I said to him, "You are the salesman. Your job is to bring in the orders, and it is somebody else's job to reject them—not you." He took the order, and the following Tuesday I owned a plane for the bid amount together with financing for two years at a 9 percent interest rate. "Butler, what have you done now?" I remember thinking to myself.

That was the beginning of accelerated growth for the company. I knew not what that decision meant at the time, but sometimes when people ask me what the best decision I ever made was at Corporex, I am tempted to say "buying the first airplane."

From 1981 to 1988, our annual billable revenues grew from $25 million to $135 million, and we grew from one office in Covington to five locations, including Tampa, Orlando, Atlanta, and Nashville. And we grew from 35 staff members to 267 salaried employees across all five offices. This was near the beginning of the migration to the sunbelt. People were moving to the sun, and business was going there as well to provide services. White collar jobs were being created in an exponential way compared to history.

During the 1980s, the airplane helped us raise $330 million in mortgage loans from 19 different banks to build more than 30 investment properties, what became known as "see through" buildings, both office and industrial warehouses. Money was flowing to support such speculation. Yet, this period was clearly our growth spurt, which propelled us into a national player. Over time, we have built or developed buildings in 27 different states.

I know for certain we could not have achieved that level of growth without the King Air. It would have otherwise been impossible to be in four cities in one day, interviewing, presenting projects to lenders, and building, and selling. The time in the air was also valuable time spent with employees—time we rarely had to socialize with each other. We often arrived home after midnight from a full day of work and were back at the office at 7 the next morning, excited to get back to work.

Although we spent a fair amount of time skipping between offices, overnight trips were infrequent, so that everyone could be home with family by night. Once you own a private jet, you work hard to keep the plane in use. Corporex's current plane is a Gulfstream G-280, which seats up to 10 people at a time. Being able to quickly move executives to the front line as needed allowed us to manage with fewer high-level managers, which is one way we could justify a plane. But planes only make sense when the company is growing.

The Name Change—Thinking Big

The year 1982 was also an important year in the company's history, because what started as W. P. Butler Company in 1970 was renamed Corporex as a strategy to unite the many companies I had established through the years that went by many different names. W. P. Butler Company was known as a construction company, and then we had OKI Realty Corp. and Acres for Industry, Inc. and American Structural Systems, Inc., which was the franchise for the metal buildings. It finally dawned on me that having a portfolio of related companies with diverse names was not the smartest way to run a railroad. I also liked the idea of choosing a name for the company that would outlast me.

The idea emerged after recognizing that customers were confused by this diversity. I'd arrive at the office of a prospective customer to market my services and I'd introduce myself as the W. P. Butler Company. And they'd reply, "Oh, the Butler Metal Building Company?" and then I'd have to take several minutes to explain who I was not, because my company was the competitor—American Buildings Company. Not a very good marketing strategy.

For that reason, and because I felt using one's own name was limiting the scope of what the company could be, we traded out the Butler name completely in 1982. We didn't hire an ad agency or market research firm for help, because we didn't have that kind of money. Instead, I brainstormed different names that would position the business as a major enterprise. The one that stood out was Corporex, which is the combination of the word corporate, to reflect our aspirations as a company, and rex, which is the Latin word for king. Together, the name Corporex means "king of companies." And the Corporex name was not limiting, not to construction, not to real estate, not to anything except business. Corporex, the company, as it turned out, has evolved and changed in many ways, been remade to respond to either changing times or changing business emphasis. But the name has never changed since that time and has become known and recognized nationally. Corporex has built buildings and developed properties in 27 different states.

Having one name as the umbrella corporation made a huge difference for the business. Then, whenever I arrived at a prospect's office and proclaimed I was from Corporex, I could explain what the company was, rather than what we were not.

It only took about 90 days for the Corporex name to catch on. People fret over changing company names, but we had the advantage of a name that was strong and visual. That name change made all the difference for our growth. We now had a brand we could build.

Corporex Gets into Banking

There was a lot occurring, not the least of which was the extraordinary 20 percent interest rate in the early 1980s. These rates and the recession of the post-inflationary period was putting a lot of pressure on the financial markets. In 1982, I was invited to be an investor in the Southern Ohio Bank, in Cincinnati. Southern Ohio Bank was, at the time, the fifth largest bank in the city, behind Fifth Third, Central Trust, First National, and Provident Banks. It was being sold by the much larger Union Commerce Bank in Cleveland, which was having difficulties due to the recession and interest rates. Southern Ohio Bank was a profitable subsidiary of Union Commerce Bank located in conservative Cincinnati, so they could offer it for sale in order to get cash back into the parent banking company.

I felt honored to be asked to participate, along with some key Cincinnati leaders, including Charlie Barrett, the chairman of Western Southern Life; Mike Conaton, president of Midland Corporation; John Strauss, Stan Strauss, Bro Lindhorst, Alan Zaring, John Davies, Manny Mayerson, and others—all CEOs. We had just formed a partnership on a building to investors of Northern Trust and raised $3.5 million dollars. I invested $1 million of that into the bank and became a board member. Not long thereafter, I was on at least two committees and had many meetings to attend. I had not planned on making such a large time commitment.

Even more interesting, around the same time period, I was asked by a mutual friend to attend a meeting with the CEO of the Federal Home Loan Bank's (FHLB) Cincinnati office. This was the federal government agency that insures the savings and loan industry. They offered me a deal they did not expect I would refuse. Well, no entrepreneurial developer would be expected to decline such an offer as this.

We met twice with the top officers of the FHLB behind closed doors in a private room at the Queen City Club; it was secret and confidential. The Federal

Home Loan Bank proposed that I merge my real estate development company, Corporex, with Home Federal Savings and Loan, a Cincinnati mutual savings and loan that the federal government wanted to take control of due to the distressed situation at the time for savings and loans. It would not cost me any money to do so, they told me, and Corporex would own the combined entity. In essence, once merged, Corporex would become the real estate subsidiary to Home Federal Savings and Loan, but I personally would own 100 percent of the institution's newly created stock in exchange for the stock of Corporex—I would own the entire merged enterprise.

Home Federal Savings and Loan in Cincinnati had $300 million in assets and Southern Ohio Bank had only $240 million, but Home Federal was a mutual savings organization. In other words, there were no shareholders. Once the merger was completed, they suggested that the new entity could then borrow, say, $20 million (a very large number for us at the time) from the federal government agency at a fixed, heavily discounted 10 percent interest rate compared to the 20 percent rates of those dire times. We could then pass along those funds to Corporex, now to be its subsidiary, and use the money to develop buildings. (Charlie Keating did exactly that with his Lincoln Savings and Loan, when he built the Phoenician Hotel complex in Phoenix and other residential subdivisions.) He asked me how that sounded. I responded, "like bread from heaven."

However, it was not long after we purchased Southern Ohio Bank that, in a special meeting, we directors were advised that nearly 15 percent of our loan portfolio at the bank was delinquent by more than 90 days. That is a big problem. Fifteen percent was more than the entire equity worth of the bank itself. Our primary customers were the milling machine industry companies, like Lodge and Shipley, Avey, and other such old manufacturing names in our community. The tool and die industry was suffering from the same extraordinary interest rates; orders for new machinery were nonexistent, and they could not pay their bills.

As a result, all of the bank directors, including me, were summoned to the Federal Reserve Bank's office in Cincinnati. While the Federal Home Loan Bank regulates the savings and loan industry, the Federal Reserve Bank regulates the banking industry. At the meeting, an officer of the Fed gave a speech about how the Fed would take control of the management decisions of the bank going forward and effectively demanded that each of us sign the single-page document that was in front of each seat. It was a consent form.

I raised my hand. "What if I choose not to sign that paper?"

The government agent rose from his chair, as if, it seemed, in levitation, pointed directly at me, and declared, "You *will* sign that paper!"

"Yes sir!" I did sign it. I also decided then and there that I would no longer entertain the acquisition of Home Federal Savings and Loan because my boss would become the federal government.

That decision turned out to be fortunate, since a number of developers nationwide took the government's offer to own various struggling savings and loan enterprises using service corporation subsidiaries like mine, and five years later found themselves in hot water—well, boiling hot would be a more appropriate representation. Federal government regulators visited their institutions and arbitrarily devalued the very real estate asset values that were contributed by the developers, meaning, the properties the government was relying on to shore up the balance sheet of the savings and loans. If the developer/owner fought back, he could find himself in jail. More than a few actually ended up there. Many lost their entire companies and worth and, moreover, their reputations.

Recently, Bill Barr, in his new book, titled *One Damn Thing After Another*, described his role as U.S. attorney general under George H. W. Bush in prosecuting more than 1,000 people in the savings and loan industry for widespread fraud that was said to have caused its collapse. However, I disagree about what or who caused the collapse. I guess events look different from various perspectives and after the passage of time.

From my perspective, it was the federal government that caused the collapse by loosening the rules and instructing savings and loan executives to diversify into commercial loans and side businesses, called "service business subsidiaries," that they were totally unqualified to deal with. Sure, there were a few cases where a bad actor took money but, based on what I witnessed and experienced, it was a series of factors beginning with inflation, high interest rates, and then the diversification ideas presented to me by the government that actually triggered it. Someone had to take the fall and it would for sure not be the government regulators. If I had gone through with the very appetizing deal they offered me, I might have become convicted citizen number 1,001 on Barr's list. I think Bill Barr is great, but he got this one wrong. But by declining to go forward with the merger, I likely dodged a bullet, a big bullet.

We shareholders ended up selling the Southern Ohio Bank to Central Trust Bank, which soon became PNC Bank, in exchange for recovering our original investment; in my case, that was $1 million, which was returned to Corporex without profit, but also without loss. It wasn't a good investment, but it certainly provided another valuable lesson, and maybe, just maybe, saved my company and myself by avoiding the savings and loan merger deal. My friend Jerry Teller often said, "Bill, you do not have those BS and MBA degrees, but you have multiple PhDs." Such lessons are what he meant. But there have been many over the years, and my goal these days is to share them with younger people to help them avoid the pitfalls.

There was another unfortunate side effect to the whole Southern Ohio Bank dilemma. The only organization I had ever really sought to be a member of is the Young Presidents Organization (YPO). To be considered for membership, you had to be the CEO of a million-dollar company and be under 40 years old, all of which was true for me. It was a mark of honor to be a member, I felt.

I was introduced to YPO by the national attorney who also represented Yamazaki Machine Tools, a Japanese company we helped to lure to Kentucky way back in 1973. So I applied to the Cincinnati chapter. A man named Tom Leyton was chair of membership. He was also the first outside president of Bishopric Products, which was owned by John Davies, one of my partners in the bank deal. John had also invested $1 million and voted a disproportionate share of the stock along with two others of us who had invested $1 million to buy the bank. Leyton called a meeting of the four special voting directors at the time Central Trust was offering to take over our bank. He put forth an alternative proposal that the four disproportionate voters buy the bank, but at the expense of squeezing out our partners and fellow board members. I would not go along with the idea because I believed that would violate the gentleman's understanding we had with the other investors when we accepted our special voting positions, even though the concept was financially appealing to a young entrepreneur like me.

For years I never understood why I was not accepted into YPO, and no one would tell me. I was well-qualified and counted many other YPO members as friends and peers. However, one could be vetoed by any other YPO member, under the rules at the time. Only many years later was it finally revealed to me that it was not a competitor who had spoken out against my application—no, it had been Tom Leyton. He retaliated for my having taken the high road on the bank deal. I still regret not having been admitted, and friends who were YPO members also felt I would have been a valuable addition. But I got too old before all this came out, and it was long ago history.

Since then, the rules have changed. No one villain can veto membership any longer. I think I could have learned a lot in the YPO programs that would have been extremely helpful to Corporex and my career, and I think I could have contributed a lot, but so be it. YPO was not meant to be. Mr. Leyton was eventually removed from Bishopric, and from Cincinnati, too.

Chapter 8

Creative Solutions to Major Problems

In 1981 I was asked to become a trustee for Thomas More College, the private Catholic-sponsored institution in Northern Kentucky. At that time, the college was in financial trouble because Northern Kentucky University (NKU), Northern Kentucky's first and only public university, had opened a beautiful new campus five years earlier and offered tuition at $1,500/year. With Thomas More's tuition at approximately $5,000, it was immediately at a huge competitive disadvantage.

This competition caused Thomas More College's enrollment to collapse, dropping from 1,300 full time equivalent (FTE) students to 660 when I joined the board.

To boost Thomas More College's financial situation, the president asked me to chair the nominating committee, with an eye to my recruiting other executives, people with money, to the board. As the custom is for board members to provide financial support, the president thought this could shore up the college's financial situation.

At the time, the budget for the school was in the range of $4.5 million annually. When I became involved, the year had just ended with $25,000 to the black; meaning, barely treading water. The only problem was that in order to balance the budget and stay out of the red, expenses had been curtailed in the extreme. As part of those measures, professors had not received a salary increase for at least five years and some of them had left. Thomas More was on the brink of failure.

I accepted the role as nominating chair, believing I could make a positive difference, and looked around the table. There were three priests, three nuns, and the rest of the members all Catholics. We needed an action board, and not just rich people, unlike the typical boards of the past. But we also needed people who could put their shoulders to the challenge.

Bishop Hughes was Chancellor, that is, chairman of the board. He was a wonderful man, an Irish graduate of Notre Dame University, who had not long ago moved to Covington from Youngstown, Ohio. He was a man of the post–Vatican II era, which was a period of great hope—for much-needed change in the Catholic Church. I asked him how he felt about adding Protestants to the board and I will never forget his answer: "We want to serve the wider community."

That was all I needed to hear. So the first three new members I brought on were a Lutheran, a Methodist, and a Presbyterian. I chose them for their shoulders, spirit, and commitment, not for their religious choice, and it turned out to be the right decision. Gradually, we replaced the priests and nuns and other former trustees—rebalancing the board—and set out to take the college forward against the odds.

Over the next 10 years, the amount of time board members contributed was incredible. While all the members played a strong part, the most energetic and committed were Bob Sathe, Jerry Thelan, Jim Bushman, and me. Other members, like John Cronin contributed in their roles but we were the unappointed or self-appointed turnaround team, so to speak. The four of us met at least two to three times weekly to develop strategies and deal with the problems for several years at least. Some of our moves were bold and creative. In the end the board upgraded the entire campus technology with computer labs, we turned surplus land into what is today a beautiful business park serving mostly healthcare tenants, we raised the salaries of teachers and professors and staff, and promised them raises every year. We rebuilt the library and added a convocation facility. At one point we went back to Bishop Hughes and asked him what would happen to the college campus and buildings if the institution failed. He said the assets would be transferred to the Diocese. My answer: "Well, you will not get them because we intend to borrow money and give mortgages to the lenders in order to fund our strategic plans."

It took 10 years, but it worked.

The biggest and best actions may have been: 1) building the Five Seasons Sports Country Club on the campus itself and thoughtfully designing the building to match the architecture of the college buildings so that from an aerial view it looked like a much bigger and attractive campus, 2) recruiting Charlie Bensman as president of the college, 3) automating a number of systems and, before I left the board, 4) started a new convocation facility, and 5) constructing the framework, the criteria and covenants, and causing improvements for 180 acres to be known as Thomas More Park, which today is a fully developed medical and professional office campus.

I left the board in 1991 not long after I was appointed chairman because at the time Corporex had fallen once again into a tough economic situation, this one would be the absolute worst of our corporate career and as in the mid-1970s, could have put us out of business.

Five Seasons is a much-improved and three times larger extension of the Northern Kentucky Indoor Tennis Club facility, which I owned in a neighboring community. I had planned to locate the new Five Seasons Sports Country Club on our 600-acre CirclePort Business Park, three miles to the east of campus, to stimulate our own development at that location. Instead, I decided to do it on Thomas More's campus to help the college. It was a double-win for the college. Thomas More would get money from a land lease, which would help the budget, and the college could offer this as an amenity in recruiting students. Once opened for use, students were permitted to use the club, two large pools, fitness, and tennis, and some had part-time jobs at the club. The first year Five Seasons opened, in 1988, the enrollment at Thomas More College increased 22 percent—in just one enrollment cycle. That was probably the biggest single incremental boost to help the college financially then, and even to date. Locating Five Seasons at Thomas

More, making it look like the college buildings was a huge contributor to the turnaround success. When I left the board of trustees during the credit crisis that followed in 1990, the enrollment was back up to near 1,100 full time equivalent students, and the operating budget had doubled. The college was on its way. Which was good news, as I had to throw all my time and energy into dealing with the incredible real estate credit crunch that was unfolding and threatening our very existence once again.

Landing Charlie Bensman as president was a major victory worth sharing. Charlie was a salesman, a charismatic personality, and a builder. We literally stole him from a similar institution in Sioux City, Iowa, called Briar Cliff University, although it was entirely a voluntary kidnapping. On a team recruiting mission to Briar Cliff, the Briar Cliff board members asked us to meet before we flew back. They wanted us to know we would not be successful in taking their beloved president; they were ready to do all they could to hold onto him. He already lived in a plush home a rich alumnus had donated, so we knew that money alone would not win his allegiance.

But we were more strategic in our approach to win Charlie over. Bob Sathe and Jerry Thelan and the recruiter took the Corporex plane to negotiate with Charlie at his college-owned mansion one Sunday morning. Sunday indeed. Having shaken hands on a deal, Bob insisted that President Bensman and his golf clubs fly with them home to Covington that very afternoon on the plane. Bob called ahead and we staged a press conference for Monday morning. It was a coup. Charlie gave an acceptance speech that morning, he was officially committed, and the local Iowa trustees never got the chance to counter our offer.

Charlie turned out to be just what the doctor ordered for Thomas More. He created a forward-leaning spirit within the institution, he increased enrollment, and for 10 years he worked hand-in-hand with the board to grow what is no longer a college but a university, now 35 years later.

Those of us who put our shoulders to that task have fond memories about what we did and all the relationships and bonds that were formed during those years surrounding this work.

The Troubled Atlanta High-Rise

An out-of-town firm is almost always considered more expert by local decision-makers than home-grown businesses. It seems the farther away the company is from its headquarters, the more respect it earns, which explains our early success in Louisville. Then, what we had done in Louisville to accelerate the company's progress we did again in Atlanta in 1986 when we took on the challenge of building the tallest building we had ever developed: 23 stories, including a five-level parking structure.

In Atlanta, a 336,000 square-foot building of that height is a relatively modest undertaking compared to the 30- to 50-story buildings that were being developed at the time. But to Corporex, it was a major project. We had never undertaken such scale in one building project, but we did it with some help.

We found a partner from Sweden, Skanska, which is a huge international contractor. Skanska was rapidly expanding into the U.S. by partnering with construction development firms like Corporex. We constructed a 50/50 joint venture and neither partner had to contribute significant cash. Corporex had already secured the site and had worked through a lot of the entitlements and plans. Together we secured a $36 million loan from First National Bank of Chicago, one of the leading banking centers in the United States, which, like so many others, no longer exists. Corporex provided all the development, construction, and leasing/marketing functions while Skanska essentially had no local responsibilities but Carl Ledjstrom, its U.S. president, was an active partner in all meetings and decisions.

From the Skanska relationship we learned about cultural differences, which we had also witnessed in the 1970s when working with a Japanese client. People of different cultures approach and interpret information in varying, and sometimes unexpected, ways.

This became clear following an engineering error that occurred during the design of the project, which was handled by our local architects and engineers. We broke ground in 1986, and construction was well underway 10 months later when our Corporex field superintendent noticed a small crack in a concrete beam in the garage of the Atlanta building. There were 37 similar joint connections in the garage, and we wanted to inspect the calculations on the reinforcing steel. The engineer and architect who worked under contract for the venture refused to provide the information. That was in itself shocking. So we hired an independent consulting engineer to review the work by reverse calculations of the structural design working from the field shop drawings, and discovered an even bigger problem related to the office tower itself. The building had been under-designed, meaning there were not enough reinforcing bars included in several highly critical areas.

The problem was huge. At the same time, we couldn't allow the issue to become widely known, since we were the out-of-towners in a highly competitive real estate developer city. We were extremely vulnerable if word got out. The problem was compounded when our partner froze the funding source from First Chicago Bank, by not signing off on loan draws. He was strategically trying to transfer the entire financial burden required to fix the problem from the partnership to Corporex unilaterally, even though the architect had been hired by both of us in the venture, and this problem was not of Corporex's making. His position was that since Corporex had recommended the architect and engineer, any problems the architect or engineer caused were Corporex's responsibility, solely, and not that of the joint venture entity. Interesting thought process, but not the correct legal interpretation, nor did it reflect favorably on the partnership we had forged.

The tab to reinforce the structure ended up costing us $800,000, and the fact that the loan draws were halted by our partner made it all very stressful. I was flying back and forth to Atlanta several times each week and Corporex ended up funding the contractors on its own until the end. Not paying the contractors on a speculative office building would damage the reputation of both the building and Corporex, prevent leasing, and we just could not let that happen.

But money was not actually the biggest problem. That was getting the building built without interruption, which became challenging after Corporex used almost all of its balance sheet cash to get to substantial completion.

Corporex tried to write a "standstill agreement" with the architect, who had hired the structural engineer, but the attorneys made a complicated mess of it. The architect was a large firm named Smallwood, Smallwood, and Reynolds AIA. We needed the architect to cooperate, continue to work, do monthly inspections, and sign off for the loan draws. They wouldn't budge. We needed a quiet solution because if the entire dispute about a structural problem spilled out into the marketplace, our competitors would have labelled the building as faulty, and we would never get a tenant to move in. I tried to tell Carl this as well when he was holding up payments to the subcontractors.

Given our inability to get the necessary understanding in a written document, I had dinner with Phil Smallwood of Smallwood, Smallwood, and Reynolds AIA and asked Phil if he was in fact a "Southern Gentleman" and good for his word, as I understood that phrase. He said with firmness, "I am." And I volunteered that I too qualified as a "gentleman," and we went on to do a handshake agreement on several material terms. We agreed that:

- We would give our word to continue to act in all situations *"as if the problem had never happened"*
- I agreed to pay his monthly fees *"as if it had not happened"*
- He would provide loan draw inspections *"as if it had not happened"*
- We would deal with all issues in the ordinary course of business until completion *"as if it had not happened"*
- And then agree to a 90-day negotiation period prior to filing any actions in court.

Corporex kept the project moving forward by investing more than $3 million of its own capital to pay the subcontractors on the job to get us to the point of substantial completion. We engaged on multiple occasions with our development partner to get reimbursed from the loan proceeds, but they turned out to be more of a hard-nosed contractor than a big picture developer. We tried a different four-point approach to resolve our differences, which was designed to give Carl a face-saving way to come around to the needed conclusion. After flying home from a failed meeting in Atlanta on a Friday, he called me to say he would accept three of the four alternate points I put forth and if I would come to his office in Greenwich, Connecticut we would solve the remainder. The only time I could do so was the Sunday morning two days later. We agreed the meeting would be at 9 a.m., so I had to leave early. He said he would bring coffee and special gingerbread cookies his wife makes each Christmas, explaining, "In Sweden, the fable goes, if you eat these cookies, they make you nice." Hmmmm!

My wife makes lots of cookies at Christmas, and on Saturday night after coming home from a party, I asked her to fix me a box of a variety of her cookies, which I took with me to the meeting. I put them on the conference table and Carl asked what was in the box. I answered: "In this box are my wife's cookies. These cookies are *cookies of understanding*. Anytime I think you do not understand me, I will lift the lid for you to eat one of my cookies."

We resolved the points of settlement that Sunday morning in Connecticut, and I wrote out in long-hand the agreement we reached on a yellow legal pad, which we both signed on the spot. This became known as the "Cookie Party Agreement." This allowed the lender to fund what amounted to most of the money Corporex had advanced. In the end, Phil Smallwood, the architect kept true to his word, as did I, and we got the building completed and certified for occupancy without the structural issue ever hitting the street, and without a written agreement.

Not long after that date, in late 1989, I decided that Corporex no longer wanted to be a partner in that venture and we negotiated for Skanska to acquire our 50 percent interest, at a loss to us. This was at the time of the start of the financial pullback, which became the "credit crunch" beginning in 1990. We didn't realize then how smart that decision to separate from Skanska and the project turned out to be, as the office market collapsed not long thereafter and didn't recover for many years. After finalizing the divorce, we closed the Atlanta office to reduce overhead expenses; we could see new financial threats on the horizon. That turned out to be an understatement.

We incurred a loss on our investment, but we gained multiple stripes on our sleeve in the form of credentials in bigger, high-rise construction work, which helped us immensely in the years ahead. We learned big lessons about the differences in thinking processes, business methods, and negotiations, all tied to the cultural differences of people from different parts of the world. We learned the mindset of the Japanese in the mid-'70s is much different than our way of thinking, and those in the Eastern bloc countries like Sweden, which is near Russia and with similar roots, is, again, different from the Japanese way of thinking. Later, we would learn about Middle Eastern cultures when we partnered with the Kuwaiti Government.

The Story that Has Never Been Told

In 1982, when short-term interest rates were approaching 20 percent, a group of four officers from Mellon Bank asked to meet with the executive team at Corporex. Based in Pittsburgh, Mellon Bank had a reputation as being a very conservative lender. We viewed commercial development of see-through buildings as anything but conservative, but Mellon wanted to lend us money for speculative development.

The Mellon team leader was Ted Miller, an executive vice president who ended up becoming a good business friend. His team of real estate pros was sharp, and I wondered why Mellon had come to us. Interest rates were off the charts, so we did not want to borrow money at 20 percent, or even at 15. In fact, I had made up my mind that I would not borrow on an open-ended floating interest rate structure that most banks offered. I considered this to be exceedingly risky. Mellon, however, told us that they had researched real estate developers in the Midwest who were expanding into the Southeast, where all of the growth action was at the time. Apparently, when we opened a Tampa office, they took notice.

What they offered us was a creative "mini-perm" (referring to a permanent interest rate for a short period of time) alternative to a pure floating rate loan, where the "constant pay rate" would be fixed at 10 percent. Actual interest costs which, at the time, were quite a bit higher, would be accrued and added to the principal balance, or credited, depending on the interest rate fluctuation above or below 10 percent. That sounded plausible to us, so we showed them four projects that were currently on hold, hoping that Mellon might be able to help with one of them.

They funded all four, to the tune of $30 million in total. That was a lot of money for us at such a pivotal time.

The period beginning shortly after 1980 was also the start of what would become known later as the savings and loan (S&L) crisis. But it was also the beginning of a bank crisis that would take longer to play out. The banking industry was bigger than the savings and loan industry, so the aggregate amount of money in play was also bigger. However, an even larger problem was forming for the financial establishment in the United States. The banks could not get loans from their regular blue-chip customers, who had found other sources of money during the high prime interest rate of the banks. Many savings and loans ultimately collapsed during the latter part of the 1980s, sooner than the banks, because they got out of their comfort zone lending to other than residential borrowers—the creative solutions on the part of their regulators. Many banks collapsed as well, but during the 1990s—the 200-year-old Bank of New England, Manufacturers Hanover Trust, Continental Bank in Chicago, and Chemical Bank all went under; really big banks, and too many to list.

After Mellon had made the first batch of loans, I happened to be playing golf with a senior officer from the bank in an outing hosted by Mellon for its real estate borrowers in Latrobe, Pennsylvania. Curious, but only six months since we closed those loans, I asked him how Mellon felt about the Corporex account. He told me that, frankly, the bank was disappointed. Why? Because we had not returned to borrow more. Mellon had anticipated, or forecast, that Corporex could borrow up to $50 million, and that is what they had intended to extend in terms of credit.

I never let our outstanding draws exceed $30 million, but his comment got me thinking. Why would a conservative bank like Mellon extend so much credit to a company like ours, with which they had no track record? To make $50 million in credit available for the asking to a smaller commercial developer they barely knew seemed unusual at best.

About 10 years later, I finally figured out why.

Mellon Bank's big borrowers in Pittsburgh included U.S. Steel, Pittsburgh Plate Glass, and many other Fortune 100 companies. These companies had lines of credit with Mellon at prime banking rates. But when interest rates skyrocketed, Merrill Lynch and Goldman Sachs and others on Wall Street arranged for these industrial companies to borrow directly from the public using 30-day commercial paper, at much lower rates than the banking industry could offer. The situation was no different for every large bank, they all had surplus money to lend. Consequently, all the big banks lost big historical accounts, because well-capitalized corporations no longer wanted their expensive money and because their company's credit worthiness allowed them to issue commercial paper directly, so as to borrow from the public rather than from the banks, and at much lower cost. It has been that way ever since.

When the Federal Reserve took steps to reignite the economy, after cutting off the money supply in 1979, it did so by shoving money into the accounts of its member banks, including, for example, Mellon, Chemical, Manufacturers Hanover, and Bank of New England. If a bank is a member of the Federal Reserve, it has no choice but to accept the money, even if it does not need it. When that happens, the banks, in turn, need to make loans to overcome the interest expense they owe the government for the unwanted money that has been deposited in their bank.

Commercial developers use big blocks of money, so the decision for all the big banks in that era, with the consent and encouragement of the federal banking regulators, was to get into the commercial real estate lending business. That way, lenders could get the money working in the quickest way possible. All the banks loaned large amounts of money to commercial developers, as well as in other industries where they could lend the most out in a short time at higher yields.

This is what then led to the savings and loan debacle. Savings and loans got into the commercial lending field, too, and had many loans go bad when the musical chairs stopped near the end of this decade. There were just too many office buildings, hotels, and retail centers built on speculation around the entire country. It all became known as the savings and loan debacle, but the problem began in the banks, not in the savings and loan industry; they had an equal, but different, problem due to the out-of-control interest rates. Because the savings and loan industry, at the direction of the government, had been making long-term fixed rate mortgages on homes, while at the same time paying a floating savings rate on savings accounts, their customers transferred their savings accounts to places where they could earn higher amounts than the savings and loan industry could offer during this excessive rate period. So the federal regulators told the savings and loans early in the 1980s that they should also make loans to commercial real estate developers. And they did, at great peril, because they understood the commercial real estate field even less than did the banking industry.

In the end, nearly all of the savings and loan enterprises were taken over by the government and given over to the bank industry or to commercial developers like Corporex. The banking industry was stronger and got a windfall in the end by adding the savings and loan industry assets to the bank balance sheets at greatly discounted pricing.

It was in an effort to save the savings and loans that the Federal Home Loan Bank also invented the idea of merging the institutions with companies like Corporex, where they could combine the net worth of our assets with those of the savings and loan institutions, such as Home Federal Savings in Cincinnati, which I mentioned had been previously offered to me.

The banking industry and the media too often faulted developers for the problems in real estate at the time that took down the banks and savings and loans, but it was the government that was pushing the money out the door into the banking centers. The amount of speculative building was incredible during the '80s. Banks were lending, savings and loans were lending, and developers were building, but tenants were becoming scarce. It all just had to come to an end, but it was difficult to foresee how until later. Being in my mid-40s, I had never lived through such an environment. I have not found that there ever was such a time unless it was the Roaring '20s.

Notwithstanding the difficulties in the financial banking industry, the 1980s were when Corporex and many other developers had big growth spurts. Revenues grew sevenfold. Corporex gathered up more than $300 million in project financing and expanded geographically at a rapid pace. Looking back, it is difficult to comprehend the energy we had.

Clearly, these were our coming out years. For all of the 1980s, more than 80 percent of our revenues were sourced in these far reaches, but by 1987 we were beginning to see signs of problems on the horizons. For that reason, beginning in the second half of the '80s we were turning our focus back somewhat from the Southeast U.S. to the rust belt, where not as much overbuild lending had been focused, and back to Greater Cincinnati.

The Grand Baldwin

The home of the famed Baldwin Piano is Cincinnati. Both the piano and the company were revered treasures in this community, a source of great pride for Cincinnatians. Today, the Baldwin Piano Company no longer exists, but its headquarters still does, because Corporex preserved this historic building and the name on it. In 1986 we acquired this stately eight-story factory, which had been converted to a headquarters structure, and repurposed it. Sometime in the 1970s, Baldwin Piano Company had become much more than a piano manufacturer. It had become a financial conglomerate of sorts under the leadership of an energetic and dynamic man named Morley Thompson. Baldwin United, as it became known, became a major Wall Street darling, with holdings primarily in the insurance industry.

Baldwin United acquired two insurance companies in Arkansas and then made a whopping big acquisition when it bought Mortgage Guarantee Insurance Company (MGIC), a 100-year-old mortgage insurer located in Milwaukee, before the incredible 20 percent interest rate period hit almost immediately thereafter. The company filed for bankruptcy when the insurance regulators would not allow Baldwin United to use reserves to meet its obligations on debt.

As part of the liquidation of the company assets, the historic Baldwin Piano building on Gilbert Avenue went up for auction.

Interstate 71, which leads from Cincinnati up to Columbus, had been built on the west side of the 11.8 acres of land previously used for warehouses and manufacturing buildings. Those industrial buildings had been razed, in fact, by a big fire years ago. I remember my dad taking me to a hill in Eden Park when I was a little boy to watch that huge fire. In the late '70s and '80s, the only building that remained was the original piano factory and headquarters of the former Baldwin United enterprise and a hole in the ground where the building's basements had been destroyed.

For years I had driven by this site and thought about its potential. Being the dreamer that I am, I had what other people might consider a crazy idea. Early in my years as an entrepreneur, I remember having the same thoughts each time I passed the site. I envisioned reversing the front of the building to face the interstate, then building a parking structure in the low-lying area below the historic building. The architecture of the original Baldwin Piano building was intact and remains to this day. It was a beautiful building, and one readily understands why we named the redeveloped project The Grand Baldwin, playing on its size and the theme of the grand piano.

We bid twice the amount at the auction that any other bidder was willing to pay. In short, the competition saw an old building that might have been convertible to apartments. But I saw an office building plus room for three or four more buildings atop the parking structures and on the surplus land across the street, on which the other bidders placed little value.

Our strategy for the signature building was to keep the best of the old and to bring the rest up to a more contemporary look, with window materials and a new monumental entrance and glassed elevators facing the interstate. This became the new front door. We built a 1,400-car parking structure in the depressed portions of the site and created a plaza complete with arboretum on the top deck. The grand opening was a first-class black-tie event; every leader in the city I could think of at the time was there. It was a grand event befitting a property that everyone in attendance was proud of.

The Grand Baldwin building was again in a somewhat pioneering location. It was neither fish nor fowl, not downtown and not in the popular suburban areas for office buildings. But to me, it was reminiscent of the very successful redevelopment area in Atlanta called Midtown. Atlanta's Midtown was just a mile or so northeast of the Atlanta central business district, and so was the Baldwin site. Identical.

The Grand Baldwin was very successful at luring tenants. We quickly drew plans for a second building atop the first garage, financed a fully speculative 10-story tower, and then eventually moved across the street to the 4.7-acre site, where we built another 1,100-car garage, a Springhill Suites hotel, a building for the headquarters of Milacron, a Cincinnati icon, and then Humana Corporation. The entire development's vision was completed, with 800,000 square feet of office space plus a hotel, and is known widely in the community as the Baldwin Center. At the same time, we were embarking on a similar scale adventure in Covington on the Kentucky riverbank.

Chapter 9

To Remake and Reimagine

The commercial development business, to a greater degree than residential, seems to lead to more business opportunities, likely because it is, in essence, the building of many businesses. Some are offices for rent, some are warehouses, and others, like retail, are natural for developers to undertake. For Corporex it was hotels and sports country clubs.

Each new development built from the ground up, as was the case with Corporex, is a new business enterprise. We get our enjoyment by building things—from office towers to business parks, which formed communities in the process. We like to talk about building people, too. In essence, we at Corporex are new business builders. Each new development is similar to a new business start-up. It takes time, often years, to ever make a profit. Yet so many people want to be developers.

I always said this is because development is like the work of God—it's about creation. And while I say it in jest, I truly believe that when we create, we are experiencing attributes that go beyond the basic human nature, maybe reaching something in us on a higher spiritual level. That is why it is fun. And even if a project should fail, done right, the property will make a lasting contribution to its environments, to its community. So there is a payback.

Being in development led us into hotels and also sports country clubs—two distinct businesses, but both requiring creativity, so to speak. The sports country clubs are novel.

Hello Hotels

In the early years of the 1980s, after we moved our offices to the Lookout Corporate Center close to the urban center, I would often visit the restaurant that revolves atop the former Quality Inn Hotel in Covington. I do not recall why I liked that restaurant so much except that it revolved; one could take in in the entire 360-degree skyline.

A younger man than I, named Dan Fay, was the food and beverage director there, and he steered a good ship. The food was good, so maybe that is why I frequented it so regularly. Dan would come around and always stop to talk and we exchanged many ideas, as I recall. But one day I recall saying to him, "If I can ever help you, let me know." I never thought any more about it, but he apparently took my statement to heart.

I think it was in 1983 he called to take me up on my offer. There was a hotel in the suburbs which he was interested in buying, but he needed a financial partner to pull it off. Together, we secured an option and while doing our due diligence learned that the accounting numbers provided to us were not correct. So we passed on that opportunity. But by then I had worked with Dan through the process, liked him a lot, knew he was a high-quality guy, and admired his desire to grow.

We were both disappointed in the outcome, so I suggested that Corporex could buy a large parcel of land on a brand new interchange under construction nearby on I-75, on which we could design a brand new state-of-the-art hotel, and Dan could manage it. At the time Middle America and the Midwest, including Detroit, Cleveland, Dayton, and Cincinnati, were disparaged as the "rust belt," a tag that persists somewhat even today. Because the region was experiencing a downturn, we at Corporex were not committing to new projects in our home port. Business activity for expansions was limited there, although the company was incredibly busy building in Florida and other parts of the Southeast. We were still stuck at the CirclePort site. Interchange access to the I-275 circle freeway in Northern Kentucky was not yet underway to allow CirclePort to flourish. Moreover, in the mid-1980s, I was already concerned about the proliferation of empty warehouses and office buildings. We had just completed our very first office building for the market and were still in the slow process of leasing it fully. We were also still leasing the Florence Space Center and the World Park industrial buildings we had completed at the turn of the decade. America's economy was still in early recovery from the outsized inflation of the previous years.

I remember thinking and saying, "Either I have to pull back or find alternatives to building speculative buildings." The access to money from banks seemed too easy; it weighed on me. I was looking for alternatives that made sense to my way of thinking, to keep the company moving forward rather than retracting. Two new sectors emerged over a period of several years as reasonable opportunities: the re-creation of the Northern Kentucky indoor tennis club into the elaborate, three times larger Five Seasons Sports Country Clubs and this new hotel program with Dan. These were two sectors where it appeared an opportunity would be prudent. Because our community had not advanced as quickly as other parts of the country, we did not yet have these services in abundance. No new hotels had been added to the Northern Kentucky population center for 10 years. Our existing tennis facility was the only one in the community. My conclusion from the study of the Ramada Inn we had optioned led me to believe that a quality void once again existed, and a void is often a sign of opportunity.

To my way of thinking, if we filled the void, we would succeed.

We were successful in securing the land and proceeded to put together an entity to build a Hilton Hotel, which Corporex would own, and another company, Commonwealth Hotels, Inc., a hotel operating venture in which Dan would have ownership and I would be the president. I would provide the lion's share of the money, the credit, the properties, and he would manage them. Well, it took two whole years to get the financing for the first one. We were turned down by dozens of lenders because we were both new to the hotel business and because the hotel was to be developed in a slow-growth geographical location.

We applied for loans far and wide and, finally, Home Savings Bank out of Kansas City indicated they would make the loan at a premium interest rate and personal guarantees on the obligation. We secured the Hilton franchise and built a beautiful 204-room hotel with an outsized dining facility and bar, too. That attachment was called the Grand Café. It took a while for the hotel to ramp up revenues, except for the Grand Café. That was a hit from the outset because Dan knew how to prepare and deliver food services. Dan and his team delivered some amazing food, started a Sunday brunch that people drove miles to frequent, and literally sold hotel rooms because people wanted to stay there for the food. The bar became the go-to place in that locale—a real hot spot. But all high-touch in every respect.

Entering the hotel business was, in many ways, another turning point for us, an expansion technically, and since then we have developed more than 40 hotels around the country. Nearly 40 years later, Commonwealth Hotels, Inc. operates more than 50 hotels around the country for Corporex and other parties. With such a large investment on our part, the hotel business became and remains a large component of Corporex's business focus and asset base. Dan Fay is still a partner, although neither he nor I are supposed to be working as hard as we do, according to what people tell us.

Five Seasons Sports Country Clubs Emerges

Five Seasons Sports Country Clubs, Inc. is another good story. It is an outgrowth of the six-court indoor tennis facility we developed on the edge of the Erlanger Crescent Springs Industrial Park, our first real estate venture. This indoor facility was an endeavor that a group of nine investors, my being one-third owner, had put together in 1973.

In 1971, Corporex had been successful in being awarded the contract to build the Eastern Hills Tennis Club in Cincinnati, and becoming familiar firsthand with the concept of indoor tennis, immediately I realized that this is something our smaller community did not have—but in my mind we needed!

So my friend Frank Sommerkamp and I gathered a group of doctors, accountants, and business executives to build a smaller facility in Kentucky. About that same time, we learned that another group of investors from Cincinnati had optioned a parcel of land further south in the Florence, Kentucky, suburbs. However, there would not be room for two such facilities in Northern Kentucky.

Within a period of two weeks, we completely designed the tennis facility with architects on my payroll and secured a building permit, since I already owned the site. We announced our plan publicly and broke ground, even though we did not have financing. In 1972 we still owned the earth-moving equipment, so I quickly began excavation and grading work in a demonstrable way. The project made the news for sure—it was a big deal at the time. No one would have doubted from examining the construction underway that this project was not a go. We secured a loan rather quickly thereafter, and the competing investor group gave up on their plan. We knew several of them, so we invited them to join our group, and three of them did just that. Their partner became the general manager. Win-win? You bet.

But like many start-up businesses with too many investors, conflicts started to emerge and the company began to suffer. After a few years, I offered to buy each of the investors' shares except for those belonging to one man, and we moved forward to turn the club around. Managing a club business is quite different than other businesses; the members want to express themselves even when they do not own or control the operations. To be successful we knew we needed to let them do that, even forming boards and committees of members so they could have their say. We learned a lot about the indoor tennis club business in the process.

One day, a general manager (GM) who had been managing the club and delivering a marginal annual profit came to my office. He was resigning for a bigger opportunity, he came to tell me. Then he told me he had appointed the tennis pro, a very young man named Kevin Molony, as general manager. This came as a surprise to me since I did not even know this young man, who was only a few years out of college. However, because the GM had been given the opportunity to participate in profit sharing in the business, he had already proceeded to sell his shares in the club, at a profit, to Kevin.

Although it is widely understood that no one should hire a "jock" to run a business, in this case, the tennis pro, we decided to give Kevin a shot. Turns out, he was good at his job. In his first twelve months on the job, Kevin, without changing the business model, increased the annual net income from $20,000 to $80,000.

I then added four racquetball courts, at his suggestion, and he then grew the bottom line to $140,000 from this small facility. We had no more land for expansion and I kept looking for a way to put more opportunity in front of this savvy athlete-turned-business executive.

He and I developed the concept of Five Seasons Sports Country Clubs, involving facilities four times larger, with swimming pools, outdoor courts, a banquet facility, restaurant, racquet ball courts, fitness center, and a spa. Our concept was to create an alternative to the golf country club and in the early years, the concept worked wonderfully.

Kevin became a life-long friend, although he ended up leaving the business over a difference of goals: I wanted to expand the business nationwide and he wanted to simply be the owner of the first facility in Northern Kentucky.

We did eventually expand to seven locations, but what happened on September 11, 2001, turned the tables on the country club industry: tax laws changed, and then other competing mega-gyms took a lot of our membership with their discounted, volume-driven offerings. The biggest, Lifetime Fitness, liked to locate within several miles of our locations, in Chicago and Indianapolis in particular.

The Towers of Rivercenter

Since its construction beginning in late 1988, the Rivercenter development in Covington, on the shores of the Ohio River, has been our most prominent endeavor. Rivercenter, now comprises six high-rise structures, three office buildings, two hotels, a world-acclaimed high-rise condominium, and a convention center. The $50 million loan we closed on in October 1988 for this project's first stage was the result of two years of effort to secure financing for an 18-story tower and an Embassy Suites hotel. It was in an urban location where no significant new commercial development had occurred for at least 70 years.

The story about how we patched leases for this project together is almost without end—we even shored up the financials for the financially strapped City of Covington in order to secure bonds for construction of the connected public parking structure. Covington, at the time, had been named by HUD as the most distressed city in the United States. Not exactly a helpful label for a place where we were trying to build an 18-story speculative high rise office building. Our loan requests on the tower and Embassy Suites Hotel project were turned down 44 times by U.S. banks, even after the First National Bank of Cincinnati had committed to sponsor the loan and actually fund 50 percent of the commitment, or $25 million. We needed bank participants for the other 50 percent and we were unrelenting and committed to getting the package together. Normally when a local lead bank is funding 50 percent, the remainder is relatively easy to secure—but not this time.

The Rivercenter development brainchild was conceived back in 1981, when Northern Kentucky's first visioning process called for a major urban landmark development. I was then vice chairman of the Governor's Economic Development Task Force, which came up with the idea as part of a grand visioning study and publication. Gordon Martin was appointed chair, but I was commissioned to lead the process. We painted a picture on the cover of the report of a dense multi-faceted complex involving office, performing arts center, and hotel. We hoped that by planting this idea in their minds, the city commissioners would not do something small with that location and waste the opportunity.

Corporex was a small company at the time, with only $25 million in revenues, and at that stage, was unable to tackle such a large project on its own. The City of Covington together with a group of the business leadership and politicos together secured an Urban Development Action Grant (UDAG), a grant from the federal government to support a riverboat entertainment facility and some part of a parking garage. Five separate commercial developers, each larger companies, were granted the exclusive development rights from 1982 to 1987, but each failed to get the development off the ground. They just did not have the necessary level of commitment and with the passage of time, the development was in jeopardy of losing the UDAG. But after seven years of rapid growth and major developments in the Southeast U.S., Corporex came back home with a much larger vision, confidence, and track record of success. Having just finished building the 23-story building in Atlanta, we felt we were ready for this challenge. And after the city commissioners had already failed five times to complete it, it was suggested that a new approach or builder might be required at this stage—even a local fellow.

Northern Kentucky was my birthplace, my community, and I was passionate about making this signature project a reality for the community. I was willing to put 25 years of work building Corporex on the line by signing a corporate loan guarantee that was big enough to bankrupt us if we did not succeed. We took on the project, pieced together 100,000 square feet of leases, which included our headquarters and a small local bank. We got the First National Bank of Covington to relocate by agreeing to buy their existing old headquarters building. We patched together leases that composed one-third of a 300,000-square-foot tower.

To this day, I am convinced that the late Ollie Waddell, then-chairman of First National Bank of Cincinnati, which he renamed Star Bank and is now part of US Bank, decided to lead this development loan for some of the same sentimental reasons that fueled my passion. Although Ollie would never admit to me that he agreed to this pioneering loan because of his early life experiences in Covington. Now that he is gone, I think I can share his story.

You see, Ollie came to Covington at the age of 13, while his mother lived in Texas. His grandmother lived in Falmouth, Kentucky, 35 miles south of Covington, which was then a long drive. So Ollie lived at the YMCA in Covington so that he could attend Holmes High School in South Covington. Why Holmes High School? Holmes High School was one of the few schools that taught Latin, which was important to Ollie's family that he study. Ollie and I had that in common, since I took four years of Latin at St. Xavier. Latin is known as a mind trainer curriculum, or at least it was back then. Great minds work together they say.

From Holmes High School, Ollie went on to the University of Cincinnati and then to Duke University before landing a job with the bank, where he spent his entire career. He had been named chairman and CEO shortly before we made our loan request.

No matter what the reason for Ollie's approval of our loan request, it was courageous on his part, given the extremely complex project involving a public garage, UDAG restrictions, bond financing, 155-year air right leases, and two buildings.

We Have Ignition!

At the time, Jeanne Schroer and I were responsible for securing financing. Today, she is CEO of the Catalytic Development Funding Corporation, but back then was a smart-as-a-whip 20-something-year-old, graduate of Indiana University, with four degrees in business, urban planning, and finance. Reporting to me, she prepared the financing presentations we made to banks and other lenders and then she and I primarily flew around the country to raise money for the 40 projects we constructed in the 1980s, including this one. She persisted with Rivercenter and finally asked a friend of hers with Canadian Imperial Bank (CBIC), which had offices in Pittsburgh, to lend us $12.5 million. CBIC agreed and introduced the project to the Bank of Nova Scotia, which lent the remaining 25 percent. We had been turned down by 44 bank lenders. It took two large Canadian banks to complete the deal.

The newspaper headlines announcing the project was proceeding proclaimed, "WE HAVE IGNITION!"

RiverCenter: We have ignition

By Greg Hartel
Kentucky Post staff reporter

Corporex Companies Inc. today launched what Mayor Denny Bowman calls "the beginning of the complete renovation of downtown Covington."

Corporex Chairman William P. Butler announced at an early-morning breakfast at the Commonwealth Hilton that the company has the financing and tenant commitments to start construction on the $80 million RiverCenter hotel/office complex.

Butler's announcement assures takeoff for a riverfront venture that has fizzled on the launching pad several times over the past decade. Construction of the hotel, office tower and parking garage along the Ohio River just west of the Suspension Bridge could begin within 30 days "if there are no snags," Butler said.

Corporex is the first in a string of developers to come up with the financial booster fuel to get the project off the ground. Covington officials and civic leaders expect it to provide the catalyst for revitalization of the city's downtown business district.

"Though it's taken a long time, your hard work will yield some accelerated fruit," Butler told Covington officials and community leaders this morning.

Bowman gave Butler a key to the city for his efforts "to make Covington a future city of new development."

The right timing and community involvement enabled Corporex to succeed where others failed, Butler said this morning. A healthy economy, interstate banking, and the expansion of Delta Air Line's hub at the airport have attracted interest the region could not draw five years ago, he said.

The other key was having a local developer with the commitment to put a lot of energy behind the project, Butler said.

Corporex announced this morning that three banks have offered to loan $20.75 million for the project, $8.25 million more than was needed to complete the financial package. The Bank of Nova Scotia, based in Toronto, committed to lending $12.5 million; Bank One of Indianapolis, $6.25 million; and Sunrise Federal Savings and Loan Association of Newport, $2 million.

Having $8 million extra in loan commitments is a "much better problem than we've had recently," Butler said.

First National of Cincinnati previously had agreed to provide $25 million and Toronto-based Canadian Imperial Bank of Commerce offered $12.5 million. Corporex and First National Bank officials will meet to work out final loan allocations so that the total equals $50 million, Butler said.

RiverCenter will include two office buildings, a 230-unit Embassy Suites hotel and a riverfront entertainment complex. The first office building will be 18 stories with 230,000 square feet of office space.

Corporex plans an ambitious 20- to 22-month construction schedule on the first office building, Butler said. "We've done it before and we're known for that."

Please see CENTER, 3K

MARK BETCHER/Kentucky Post illustration

Construction on Covington's RiverCenter complex should begin this year now that developers have secured the loans needed to build the project. RiverCenter will include a 230-suite hotel atop a 900-car parking garage, two office towers and a floating entertainment center. Nearby property also has been targeted for future redevelopment.

Finally time for genuine excitement

By Michael Collins
Kentucky Post staff reporter

Butch Callery watched for more than eight years as developers paraded before the Covington city commission with plans for a hotel-office complex along the Ohio River.

Each time, city officials and community leaders greeted the developers with a great deal of excitement and fanfare. Each time, financial obstacles or other problems dashed the optimism.

Callery, who is beginning his ninth year as a commissioner, hesitated to join in the hoopla. "I thought it was going to take some time, and I was willing to wait," he said.

The waiting paid off this morning when Corporex Companies Inc. announced it has secured financing for the $80 million RiverCenter hotel-office complex. Callery expects the project to take shape now that Corporex has secured financing.

He attributes Corporex's success to "good old-fashioned, roll-up-the-sleeves hard work." And he can't keep from getting caught up in all the commotion.

"I'm real excited," Callery said. "This isn't something that is going to sit there another four or five years. We're going to be moving on it this year."

Supporters and skeptics alike said the announcement is probably the most significant news for the city since plans for the project began nearly a decade ago.

"I'm delighted," said Frank Sommerkamp, an employee of Cincinnati Bell and community leader. "We have all been holding mental hands with Corporex since it became the master developer.

"Each time we got closer to

Please see EXCITE, 3K

It was an exciting time for our small community of Northern Kentucky. The Canadian bankers had a different perspective on the project, thank goodness. Where all the U.S. banks rejected the loan because it was viewed as pioneering, the Canadians saw it as a void that needed to be filled. A pioneering perception is often, in reality, a vacuum, where a need was unserved. That turned out to be the case here.

It has always been the Corporex way to seek out a service that was not adequately or professionally addressed, and to design a way to fill the gap. That is what made us successful in providing turnkey design-and-build services. That is what satisfied the vacuum that existed in Northern Kentucky, which we are still striving to fill.

The legal documentation was difficult and trying, because the attorneys and others associated with the City of Covington were literally scared, due to the magnitude, complexity, and risk, which they deemed to be substantial. So too was the attorney for the lenders. For that reason, it took eight months to pull the deal together to close the loan. Then, the closing took eight hours, because of all the documents to be signed.

After all the documents had been signed, everyone at the table looked to me. I was frustrated and, without exaggeration, I was simply exhausted by the whole two-year experience, which required my constant energy and attention. As I got up from hours of document signing, I remember exactly my statement to those around the table: "Usually the developer takes everyone who was involved out to dinner after the closing, to celebrate. But I just don't feel like it! This deal did not have to be this difficult." I was upset with a number of people there who had made the deal harder than necessary to close.

I told the group, "I'm going home and if, after reflection and some time passes, if I feel better about it, we'll put together a dinner." And then I left. I never scheduled that dinner.

As I walked to my car, through downtown Cincinnati, my brother Marty, who was the real estate attorney who had been instrumental in solving many complex issues associated with the deal, joined me. "How do you feel?" he asked. And I will always remember my response, which was, "*Corporex may not be here in five years, but I know we can get those structures built, and they will be here for 200 years.*" And that was okay with me, quite honestly. Contributing to the city's skyline was more important than lining Corporex's coffers, and always has been.

Leasing the office building was indeed a challenge. Getting industries to relocate to Covington took time. But eventually, we were able to sign headquarters tenants, including Ashland Oil, Xpedx Basis Burke Marketing, Gibson Greeting Cards, and Omnicare—and then, of course, Rivercenter became and remains the headquarters for Corporex.

It took three and a half years from the opening date in 1990 to break even on cash flow. In total, it took seven years to get the business up and running, two years up front getting leases and financing, then 18 months of construction, and then three and a half years to get enough leases to pay the loans and operating costs. This illustrates what the development business is all about, and the long-term commitment needed to succeed. But since the first buildings, we have added four more major structures to Rivercenter and worked with Kenton County and the Commonwealth of Kentucky to add a 1,500-car parking structure and a state-of-the-art convention and conference center to the neighborhood.

The convention center enabled the building of three more developments: the Marriott Hotel, Madison Place offices, and the high-end residential condominium towers.

My good friend, the late Bill Keating, named it "Butlerville."

When I look back over the decade of the 1980s, the explosive growth, hiring more than 200 people, serving on the bank board, volunteering with Thomas More College, growing to five offices from one, undertaking the high-rises in Atlanta and Covington too, closing all those loans, and at the same time, building blimp hangars and multiple industrial buildings around the country, and then the serious problems we encountered, it is mind boggling. Where did all that energy come from? Was I ever home? Even if I was at home, was I actually there? I did try to be.

In order to spend more good time with Sue and the kids, I bought a cabin down on Lake Cumberland and a ski boat. Every Friday in the spring and summer, Sue and I would load up the car with Kevin and Christa as early as possible in the day, to head three hours to the lake. Getting in the water helped me disconnect from work (a little) and it was a good time swimming and skiing as a family. Sue does not swim, but she drove the ski boat for us. However, my briefcase and the yellow legal pads on which I wrote constantly were always present. The kids to this day tease me about the yellow legal pads.

Time for Reckoning

Again, the end of the 1980s, following the period of excessive lending, was hell at best. Real estate had been overbuilt across the board, from office to industrial to retail and hotels, thanks to the banking industry at the behest of the federal government, culminating in a huge economic problem which was not yet understood. During the latter 1980s, I wondered when this craziness would stop, the lending would come to a halt and no more "see thru" buildings would be developed.

I had stopped in at Christmastime 1988 to have a drink with Larry Hurd, chief real estate loan officer for First National Bank of Florida in Tampa. We met in the bank's corporate dining room and he told me how the Office of the Controller of the Currency, one of three supervising regulatory agencies of the U.S. government, had been camped out in the bank for the previous six weeks. They were focused in the real estate department, writing down the values of the loans outstanding on the bank's books, causing his bank to record financial losses against its income, a serious matter. Larry told me that they had departed the previous Friday and on Monday, the next working day, and without notice, a SWAT team of another agency of the government, the Federal Reserve Bank appeared unannounced and began examining the real estate loans once again. And again, the real estate lending department of the bank was thrown into turmoil and frustration. Larry's story scared me.

I put two and two together. I quickly figured out how the U.S. government regulators intended to put a stop to the over-lending and overbuilding of speculative buildings—through intimidation! By chastising the bank officers and writing down appraisal values on property and loans to the point that no sane banker would make another loan, the government would now reverse the looseness they themselves caused—by instilling fear. Thus began the severe period that became known as "the credit crunch." Use of the term severe is indeed appropriate, even understated, for the years that followed.

From this day forward, developers like us could not refinance our loans or find a way to repay them on the maturity date. We were totally cut off from any type of lending. It is difficult to find the words that could properly convey the gravity of an event when absolutely no financial support is available to an entire industry, or to fully convey the level of emotional stress that occurred. The "credit crunch" as it quickly became known was another first for us, maybe a first in the history of America except for the Great Depression of the 1930s.

The financing of Rivercenter and Baldwin II, we decided, were our last new deals before taking defensive measures. Many new projects were coming out of the ground yet in 1991, at least in our Middle American states. By acting early, within 100 days of my meeting with Larry Hurd, Corporex was able to survive what came next. Actually, I had sensed a downturn, as I had begun clipping news articles from the *Wall Street Journal* and other business publications months before that had raised my antennas. (I have a portfolio of them.) It seems that being a visionary can also be helpful in seeing danger ahead; that was certainly the case here.

Not many developers made it through the credit crunch to follow.

Chapter 10

All Growth Happens out of Difficulty

It was also in the 1988, as we were trying to monetize assets, that we met the Fosterlane Management Company, which was owned by the sovereign Middle East country of Kuwait. It was their U.S. real estate investing arm. Kuwait had many investments in office buildings in the U.S. but wanted to begin investing in industrial buildings.

The Kuwait Government Partnership—Wars Have Extended Outcomes!

In 1990, executives at Fosterlane Management suggested they would be willing to partner with us for the development of large industrial buildings in the United States. By June 1990, we had negotiated to contribute a 250,000 square-foot building we already owned in Orlando to the partnership and to immediately build 500,000 square feet more as part of a 750,000 square-foot complex on added land we owned. This was a very large investment back then.

Fosterlane committed $21 million to fund the venture, which was fortuitous, since they had money and the project would have no mortgage debt. For a company like Corporex during a period when cash was precious, this was a Godsend. Fosterlane would own 70 percent and we would own 30 percent. The agreement was that we would do all the work and manage the partnership autonomously, and that we would not reference Kuwait at all, as they liked privacy. There was nothing wrong in doing this and there was nothing unethical about it, that was just their policy. They were very selective about their partners. Gerald Hines, one of the most highly regarded developers in America, was their other partner in the United States and he built office towers. They had six towers at the time in New York City, like the Lipstick Building on Third Avenue, but people only knew those properties as owned by Gerald Hines Interests.

We could not have anticipated what happened next. Just two months after closing the deal in June of 1990, on August 11, Saddam Hussein of Iraq attacked Kuwait, causing the project funds to be frozen. Fortunately, they were released after 90 days and we kept the project moving during the Gulf War. However, after the war ended, and just as we were seeking tenants for the buildings and in the middle of the real estate credit crunch, the top execs of Fosterlane in the U.S. were abruptly terminated and a new CEO installed. He was Saleh Alzouman, a Kuwaiti national by birth, who had been on the board of directors of Fosterlane. He was a character without creed.

He quickly cut off the funding we needed to complete the buildings in an effort, we learned later during litigation, to squeeze Corporex out of ownership so that Fosterlane could sell the property and recoup money that it could send back to Kuwait to help repay its war obligations. It would have been helpful if he had just stated that; we could have worked together to help their problem.

However, we only learned this in depositions years later—moreover, the parliament of Kuwait had been disbanded by the royal family before the war, which makes one wonder if that had anything to do with the invasion by Iraq, but then reconstituted afterward because the war itself had diminished the royal family's power. Everything changed for us because of the Gulf War. Corporex was one of the victims. But we were in control of the property for the first five years, until 1995, and they could not force us to sell or give our ownership over to them as he suggested once in a meeting.

So they froze the funding, which was a breach of the joint venture agreement. We were at a stalemate, which then moved to litigation in Orlando. It was there that, during a deposition of Mr. Alzouman, when he was embarrassed by our questions about why he is not, after 20 years, a citizen of the U.S., he asked to pause for negotiations. I then made an offer: Give us six months to acquire their 70 percent interest, and to recoup his investment back in full, which was approximately $18 million at that point. If we failed in that period, Kuwait could buy our 30 percent share for $1 million.

He took it. We then spent many hours getting the written agreement in order and legally binding. We signed it after midnight and did not board the plane to return to Covington until 2 a.m. the following day. I remember being elated, and punchy. Elva Malott, my long-term executive assistant, was with me. I remember dictating a crazy letter with her help to all the attorneys and others involved, describing a boxer: "There he stood in the ring, his arms limp at his side." Alzouman had conceded.

Some months later, when we finally sold the buildings, the lawyer who represented us flew to Covington with a trophy they had created to commemorate the transaction. I know not where they found the boxer standing with his defenses down, but it is perfect. And fun.

Ultimately, what happened was that we sold the property within the promised six-month window. In another room down the corridor on the same day that it sold, we paid Kuwait the $18 million it was owed from the $24 million we received in funds from the sale. The remaining $6 million in profit came at a critical time for us as we were still in recovery mode from the recession. . . . It wasn't a bad deal, especially since we were just coming out of the credit crunch, but still less than what might have been had the timing been different. The original intent was for this project to be the first of many such large industrial buildings for Corporex to build in partnership with Fosterlane Management's pension funds throughout the U.S. We were lucky to have made any profit at all, considering the timeframe, but the Gulf War had turned everything upside down and scuttled what should have been, would have been, a huge opportunity for Corporex over time. Unfortunate, but I guess wars affect small companies sometimes, too. Not too many companies like ours experience the trauma of a war's impact, that is for sure. And this event happened during the most difficult years of our corporate career, putting added pressure on our cash flows.

The Horrific Credit Crunch

The period from 1990 to mid-1995 was another time when we should have been out of business by most financial standards. At one point during that period, we had essentially run out of cash and were behind in interest payments on loans to the extent of $6.5 million. We were not alone; very few of our peers in development were able to survive this devastating experience.

I had thought the very first recession we lived through was the worst until this came along. I have often referred to the 1973–1975 oil-induced contraction by speaking to a soft spot in the back of my head. It is automatic for me to reach with my hand to that area when describing that recession, the location of which for whatever reason is on the left side of my skull.

But the first recession we lived through proved to be a mild event compared to what occurred later, following the savings and loan debacle of the late 1980s. It is difficult to adequately explain the impact a total credit freeze has on a commercial real estate business when it lasts for five years. From 1986 to early1989, we had added an average of $100 million annually in new project debt. But from 1990 to 1995 we were unable to borrow even a dollar, until lending ultimately reactivated. The pain was profound. Many banks and savings and loan institutions failed in this period, and only one in eight commercial developer peers survived.

Without outside financing, Corporex had to push through to the other side solely on the strength of our assets, and we did. Our properties served us well—better than most developers because we had been so diligent about reducing the costs during initial construction, and because we had leased selectively to quality tenants. But the period that followed was not without extreme pain and extraordinary actions. It felt like we were once again tearing down the company we had built, just as we had done in the mid-1970s.

One of my oft-repeated statements is "quality has never failed us," and that was never more true or important during the credit crunch of the early 1990s. We always added extra features to enhance the quality and appeal of our properties.

Because our costs to construct were lower, our loan amounts were correspondingly lower per project than our peers. That helped a lot. Our lease documents were written better and often the rental rate we achieved was better because we sought only quality tenants who were attracted to our higher quality products. We reduced our overhead during this period as much as we could afford to cut, without impacting the quality of services provided to our tenants. But the toughest challenge was the need to reduce overhead costs by reducing our employee headcount. Had we not had the foresight and the willingness to be decisive early on, we would not have survived the period that followed. Not that it was easy, because it wasn't. It was painful. We had to reduce our payroll from 267 salaried people to 77, closed offices, negotiated our way out of the Atlanta partnership and closed that office, negotiated various loan extensions to weather the storm, even deeded several properties to lenders in exchange for debt forfeiture on their part in cases where the lender actually preferred that solution and we were willing to comply.

Corporex had already acted several years earlier to aggressively reverse our focus from new development in the Southeast U.S. cities back to our home-base—back to the middle-American cities, the rust belt areas of Cincinnati and Kentucky, which were not so overbuilt. That foresight again paid off.

In October 1988, we had closed on $80 million in new loans projects in Greater Cincinnati alone, an integral part of our strategy to flip our efforts back into the local markets from the southern states. The Towers of Rivercenter office building and the Embassy Suites Hotel, a loan on Baldwin 200 in Cincinnati, and an industrial building near the Greater Cincinnati/Northern Kentucky airport were all announced in one month. The local media wrote articles that painted Corporex as lighting rockets. No one developer had attempted anything so audacious in this Greater Cincinnati community. But we were already carrying out the strategy in advance of the perceived storm. Around June 1989, only eight months after we announced those large speculative buildings and before the credit crunch became generally recognized either by ourselves or others in banking, we executed on a decisive fail-safe strategy involving serious staff reductions and other measures, closed Atlanta and Nashville operations.

Our very early actions, beginning in 1988, had also included selling assets to get ready for whatever lay ahead. Concerned about a hypothetical pending crisis, we had begun the process of trying to sell assets to build liquidity, and did so with partial success. In late 1989 or early 1990, we sold a portfolio of industrial buildings to Equitable Life and put significant cash in the bank. We had tried to sell a much larger package of buildings, but, in retrospect, the markets were already weakening. At the end of that year, 1990, we had $10.7 million of free and clear cash on the balance sheet. It was not in my mind the war chest I sought, but in the end turned out to be enough. But by February of 1992 only 14 months later, we had only $200,000 left, not enough to make the checking accounts work. That is how bad it got during the credit crunch. Cash was rolling out at an unheard-of pace. Having that cash on hand at the beginning of the cycle, combined with our efforts to reduce operating overhead, and then to extend and re-structure loans made all the difference. Again, we had been visionary and out of sync with everyone else it seemed. I remember meeting with a lender bank in Cleveland in 1991, showing them our negative forecast of the future, and he did not buy into the looming problem picture I was painting. He said, “Corporex looks fine. Let me lend you more money to reinforce your balance sheet.” I already would have nearly $350 million in mortgage debt outstanding, once all the new loans became fully funded, and just did not want any additional debt obligations. But at the time, neither he nor we knew the full extent of the boycott on commercial developers.

Had we not implemented the fail-safe plan fully, when we did, we would not have survived this period—of that, I am sure. It was indeed visionary, triggered by one meeting with the banker in Tampa and my own study of the looming economic contraction—and my immense fear of failure. But, again in retrospect, the handwriting was on the wall at that point, which I gleaned from all the news articles I had been reading and clipping about overbuilding and the savings and loan problems. The aggregate formed a catalog of facts that pointed to trouble. The meeting in Tampa with the banker only confirmed what I had suspected, what I had been feeling, though I didn't know how it would unfold and when. But by preparing for what we were fairly certain was to come, we saved Corporex when 85 percent of our peers failed.

That five-year period was the most stressful, difficult time in our history—even worse than the oil embargo of the 1970s, because at least that particular recession was short-lived. During the Great Recession that occurred 19 years later, starting in 2008, bankers would say to me when referring to the current financial situation: "This is the worst economic period you have ever seen, is it not?" And I would simply shake my head and say, "No, not even close," thinking of the incredible credit crunch experience. When I think back over this event I wonder, what if we had not sold that portfolio to put $10 million in the bank? Or, what if I had not stopped in to have a drink with the banker in Tampa? Someone was watching over us, and frankly that has always been the case.

When this debacle was finally behind us, sometime in the latter part of the 1990s, I wrote what we dubbed "The Developer's Insurance Policy." I have it framed and hanging on my office wall as a reminder to me and all the Corporex officers ever since. The inscription:

- Never sign personally
- Never cross-collateralize
- Never second mortgage
- Build inside a corporation
- Don't over-borrow
- Don't put all your eggs in one basket

- Don't borrow from only one source
- Lease high to credit tenants

We know for sure that these principles are what made the difference, allowing us to survive this period when only a 13 percent of entrepreneurs in our business nationwide, as Barry Manilow sang, "made it through the rain . . ."

It was in the middle of this incredible stress-filled downturn that I learned one of the most valuable lessons of my life. Bishop William Hughes was the leader of the Catholic Diocese of Covington at the time and also the chancellor of the board of Thomas More College, which I wrote about earlier. In addition to being a spiritual person, he was also a smart man with a mild and pleasant demeanor. He and I were having a phone conversation in which I was asking him to introduce me to a person of financial means whom he knew. Bishop Hughes had come to our diocese from Youngstown, Ohio, and knew Ed DeBartolo Sr. personally; at the time I was grabbing at straws to find any avenue to get relief from our severe financial problem. As I was sharing our plight with Bishop Hughes, I must have become quite emotional as I unknowingly unloaded my frustrations. In all the many years I knew and worked beside him at the college, I had never heard Bishop Hughes raise his voice, not over any situation. But he did this one time: "Bill! Bill!" he said in a strongly raised tone, and I stopped talking. "Don't you know? All growth happens out of difficulty!"

I think that was the end of the conversation, but not the end of the message, which has rung in my memory ever since. All growth happens out of difficulty. So it is, and I came to understand that the growth is not in the difficulty, but rather in how we embrace the situation and accept the difficulty as an opportunity to rise up. The growth is in our response to the difficulty when we reach out for help, sometimes from our relationships, but sometimes from our God. And I came to understand that in reaching out to the Source of life, we find inner strength, and we find spiritual growth. While there were more lessons learned from Bishop Hughes, for me, this one lesson is worth all the work and contributions I made to the college over 10 years, because in that process I came to know a great man. He now lives in peace.

There were many actions taken over multiple years to overcome the challenging events of that era, but I wonder sometimes whether we could have survived when so many others did not, had we not been people of faith who were willing to reach for the extra strength so needed in such times.

How I Won National Entrepreneur of the Year: 1996

In 1996 I received what is yet today my most valued secular honor. I have since received many highly acclaimed awards of recognition, but most came later, such as "Great Living Cincinnatian." But at the time, and still today, to be named National Entrepreneur of the Year is a big deal for a guy like me who started with nothing. The award was made by the Master of Ceremonies Lou Dobbs in Palm Desert, California, by the co-sponsors of this very coveted recognition: Ernst and Young CPA, The Kaufman Foundation, CNN, and Nasdaq. The award is given annually at a huge ceremony after a lengthy process of elimination that begins in large cities, then regions, and is then judged by a national panel.

One of the award's judges told me that my story about how I opened an office 100 miles away in Louisville at the age of 25, because I could not win a contract to build a building in my smaller hometown, was pivotal to their choosing me as the most qualified.

Receiving this award, so rare among so many entrepreneurs, felt like the capstone of my career, at least to that point on the journey. I found my acceptance comments worth sharing:

> "If we are so fortunate to find ourselves in America; then gifted with visions and dreams, and the ability to follow those dreams; and on top of this we are touched by God and thereby know love; then we have the grand opportunity to experience life in its fullest.
>
> It is in following those dreams, sometimes undertaking serious risks for sake of the mission, that we make a difference; and in so doing live life in a very full manner.
>
> And for this you call me an entrepreneur and honor me, and I accept with sincerity. But no man is an island!"

And, of course, I shared the honor with my associates who, through their commitments and contributions, had helped to make Corporex and myself award-winning. I thought they should have ownership in that honor.

Quest

It was in the middle of the 1990s that the board of directors of the Tri-County Economic Development enterprise called me to a meeting. The formation of a unified three-county economic development vehicle was an outcome of one of the 16 recommendations put forth in "Northern Kentucky's Future," the publication I authored in 1981 along side a group of entrepreneurs that included Gordon Martin, Dennis Griffin, Matth Toebben as part of John Y. Brown's appointed Governor's Economic Development Task Force. Since most of those 16 actions had actually occurred, and this vision publication had been surprisingly successful, they asked if I would chair a new visioning process again.

In order for this not to evolve as another Bill Butler idea, we asked the president of Thomas More College at the time, Father Bill Cleves, to co-chair. He agreed. We made a good team and he and I maintain a close relationship to this day. Together, we tackled a robust agenda over a two-year period involving the whole community, gathering input from more than 2,000 residents.

The plans that resulted were received with much enthusiasm—indeed, with excitement. A board called Forward Quest was formed to take the vision and projects within to fruition, to implement the programs. (QUEST is the name of the publication describing this visioning work outcome, it is much more in-depth and broader and more reaching than the "Northern Kentucky's Future" publication.)

Unfortunately, the group which applied for the task of taking the Quest vision forward and were named to that board did not follow through well, what was accomplished over the next 10 years was minimal. They were community leaders in diverse ways but, in hindsight, they did not have a vested interest or motivation to cause true progress, at least not at the level that is required for such undertakings. Quest was an intense and comprehensive work which should have moved the community even further than the first plan. But that did not happen. However, the visioning effort was not wasted, and through that process itself, many others enhanced their own knowledge and vision of what the Northern Kentucky of the future could look like. Some of this energy remains active yet today, 25 years later.

Many of the Quest ideas remain valid and timely, even to this day, and could still be implemented. I was exhausted at the time and chose not to join the new board, but undertook one of the Quest projects, which was to form the "Metropolitan Growth Alliance." Its goal was to reach across the river and engage both Cincinnati and Northern Kentucky into an educational and unifying long-term effort. Our goal was to advance what we coined the 360-degree region of 1.8 million people into a process that would move us forward step-by-step with more oneness. I know this. Finding a way to collaborate and present a unified sense of place is ultimately the key to unlocking success for this metropolitan center in a globally competing economy.

Once again, two things happened to impede that program: 1) I became embroiled in an egregious attack on Corporex and myself over a government contract for three buildings in Kenton County, and 2) some of the old guard in Cincinnati hijacked the Metropolitan Growth Alliance movement itself and diverted the effort to the point that it did not exist for long thereafter. Someday Cincinnati will come to the realization that the fast-growing population center to the south in Kentucky is essential to the quality of life of the larger region. It currently represents 22 percent of the Greater Cincinnati population. Perhaps when that realization happens, there will be a recognition that Northern Kentucky is actually quite sophisticated. Maybe then there will be a determined effort to find a way to truly "bridge the bridges," at least with respect to joint economic and community growth and development aspirations.

A Big Idea

There is one project in Quest depicting a monorail that circles the entire Cincinnati-Northern Kentucky urban river zone with an arm, an extension to the airport. This one concept would do more to solve the geopolitical problem than any other; it would paint a progressive picture on an otherwise complacent image. It is a bold and progressive concept that does not have a competitive component—both Cincinnati and Northern Kentucky would benefit. An elevated rail that loops the areas around the sports stadiums in Cincinnati and around the major riverfront developments in Covington and Newport would be a huge marketing tool for Greater Cincinnati's image in the world. It would be intriguing, and it is quite feasible. Parking structures in this particular area could be better utilized because people could get on the loop rail and park in Kentucky in order to attend the Bengals or Cincinnati Reds sports activities. The loop rail could also include a spur to our international airport. This would tie the international airport, located in Kentucky, to the core of the entire community. It is a novel idea with a lot of merit, if only the region could secure cooperation from state government in both Kentucky and Ohio. Such is certainly possible.

Chapter 11

Victory of Truth, Work, and Prayer

If you have ever been the target of a grand jury investigation, you know more about yourself than 99 percent of the people in the U.S. It is a horrible experience, one which even to this day I do not know why it happened, but it did.. Oh, I know the particulars of what occurred, but I have yet to understand the message or lesson, if any, that I was to garner from the experience. I know that coming out the other end I was changed, and the way we do business changed, but to what extent is hard to describe. One thing is for sure: we have for years avoided any similar contracts with government agencies due to their inherent adversarial political downside.

What happened could be an entire book on its own, it's so involved. I have avoided writing about it or allowing others to do so because certain people would be hurt by the revelation of their devious conduct. They might deserve the revelations, but still. And exposure is not my intent here, yet the story of Corporex and important lessons worth sharing would not be correct or complete without some mention of this incredible 18 month saga.

The ordeal began when the County of Kenton took turnkey bids for the design and construction of a big parking structure and new Justice Center office building at Rivercenter in Covington. The garage was developed in conjunction with construction of the new convention center by the State of Kentucky, which we had been instrumental in securing for the community. Corporex did not typically entertain public bid work, but since we had recently completed a beautiful dual-government building project in Hamilton, Ohio, that involved a large justice center and both county and city headquarters—strikingly similar to the Kenton County project—we decided to participate. Moreover, I wanted to ensure, if possible, that the architectural quality of these buildings met our high standards for the Rivercenter neighborhood that we have developed. Our designs provided a great deal of architectural appeal that the other bidders did not offer. We were willing to forgo profit to get good-looking buildings. The Hamilton, Ohio project was very successful, and the elected official present at the ribbon-cutting stated that Corporex had saved them roughly one-third of what other recent projects had cost throughout Ohio for such judicial centers. Based on that information, we believed we could be successful here, too, and render a quality service as well. We helped Kenton County set forth the specifications that set the minimum standards. The government employed an independent architect to scope and oversee the entire bidding process.

Three companies bid and Corporex's bid, which was the lowest with the most robust plan, was unanimously selected by the commissioners. That is where the trouble began.

Unfortunately, one of the companies that had submitted a bid was upset at not having been awarded the project. The owner of Wessels Construction apparently thought he had the inside track, perhaps thanks to a close personal relationship with the chief administrator of the county who also supervised the bid process. It was the administrator, not the elected executive, who then decided after the public bid openings to refuse release of the plans or bids to the media. He said this was no longer an open bid situation but a "competitive negotiation," harking to a different provision in their code. He changed the foundation of the process. But the bids had already been opened in a public forum. His refusal to release the bids to the public immediately created an air of suspicion. Why wasn't he sharing them, people murmured? What was being hidden? The commissioners voted to award to Corporex.

Wessels Construction filed suit against the county government, and the saga grew from there. Other commissioners from the opposite political party to that of the elected County Judge Executive saw this as an opportunity to attack him, and accuse him of collaborating with Corporex, despite the fact that the bids were all opened and read in public. There had been no opportunity for back-door dealings. With little else newsworthy to report on, the local media fed on the situation and printed the allegations and accusations, something almost every day, adding fuel to a fire where there was really no smoke at all.

What should have been dismissed grew into what the press next labelled a "scandal," complete with an in-depth investigation of the bid process. The newspapers were having a field day; there was an article stirring the pot each and every day. In the meantime, the work proceeded and the projects were completed even before the litigation issues were settled. We had never experienced a situation where the facts and the truth did not carry the day; but it seems this is now much more common today. In order to get the facts out to the public, we printed our own newspaper look-alike, and mailed it widely. In the end truth did prevail.

Although Corporex was not specifically named in the initial lawsuit with the county, we were continuously—daily—mentioned in the news related to the ordeal. Eventually, under much pressure and a trumped-up threat that he would lose his state pension if he were found guilty of anything, the Judge Executive resigned. At the age of 72, he had intended to retire in five months anyway, but on bad advice from counsel he accelerated his resignation. In that same meeting where he announced his resignation, the commissioners approved paying the losing bidders a total of $800,000—one losing bidder got $500,000 and another who had piled on when he heard there might be a settlement, received $300,000.

That did not make any sense at all, except that there was a power play underway on the part of people of the political party opposite the Judge Executive to oust him and to name a replacement of their choice, rather than one elected. In order to deflect their bad conduct in the public eye, the guns were turned on Corporex with an action to get us to reimburse the money that had been promised the losing bidders. We refused, making it clear that there was no cause for these allegations.

The county attorney, who originally defended the county's handling of the bidding process and awarding the contract to Corporex, switched sides for his attorney friends.

Corporex fought the lawsuit, which was a civil action, aggressively, and in the course of litigation, collected significant evidence of the internal events leading up to the Judge Executive's resignation. The matter went on for a long time—18 months of gathering facts to support our innocence. It was a good thing that we fought to preserve our reputation, and, moreover, that we could afford to do so.

The group behind this misconduct was able to get their friend, the Kentucky State attorney general, to convene a grand jury for the sole purpose of putting more pressure on us, and in particular me, to settle the matter. Forming a grand jury was serious; elevating the fight to a criminal level was in their minds a threat that a businessman could not risk. It was serious, and some of my closest and most respected business friends actually conducted an intervention to convince me to settle, in the face of some felony indictment for which there was no basis in law. But grand juries can do just that—indict even when there is no proof of wrongdoing. If I did settle, it would be construed by the public as an admission of guilt. I learned this: in a criminal indictment, the defendant cannot take depositions of witnesses or gather facts under oath. That is not fair. The accused in a criminal process is critically disadvantaged in mounting a defense of themselves.

But we were able to secure evidence from witnesses under oath only because the county's financial claim against us was a civil court action, not criminal, and this effort on their part to deflect the blame foiled the plaintiff's actions in the end. We were able to collect a massive amount of testimony from the county commissioners themselves and other witnesses under oath that exposed the entire plot. The grand jury was essentially a politically motivated sham jury seated to put pressure on Corporex under the threat of a criminal indictment for a poorly written and undefined section of the code styled "abuse of public information."

We fought in court on principle, as well as for cause, and somewhere late in the process I came up with an idea. I proactively secured notarized and witnessed affidavits from three of the independent architects who were involved in the project bidding, all of whom voluntarily executed the exact same sworn statements that affirmed: 1) They had participated in many public bid openings as professionals 2) They were each present when the bids were opened and read aloud, and 3) The bids were opened in public and therefore available to everyone and anyone. The affidavits included one from the architect hired by Wessels, the plaintiff, the very contractor that filed the first action, as well as from the very architect who was employed by the county government itself to supervise the bidding process for the sole purpose of ensuring the proper handling of the bids on behalf of the county. In those affidavits, not one but three separate and independent architects confirmed that there was nothing underhanded about the bid or selection process.

These affidavits were never made public. The timing was the very week that I was to be indicted. I know this because the plaintiff's attorneys who were coordinating with the attorney general's gunslinging prosecutors leaked their plan to the press. I had a few connections of my own and I was able to put together the pieces of their plan, which were later confirmed. In preparation to defend Corporex and myself, I had hired a prominent criminal attorney located in the Kentucky state capital. That too was pivotal. Big Bill Johnson, as I called him, could literally walk around to the office of the attorney general in Frankfort. So I instructed him to hand one copy of the architect's sworn affidavit to each of the prosecutors involved, including the attorney general himself, if present. I did not send all the affidavits at the same time. Strategically, we delivered six copies of the statement from the first architect, the one who designed our buildings, on Monday of that fateful week, and then waited two days. Then we delivered six copies of the affidavit of the county's own consultant architect who had overseen the bidding process on Wednesday, and waited. The indictment did not arrive as they had planned. And finally, two days later on Friday we delivered six copies of the sworn statement from the architect who was employed by the actual instigator who claimed foul, Wessels Construction. That one sealed the deal. The attorney general must have wondered what was coming next, and knew then and there that if he pursued this unfounded action further, he would be embarrassed in trial with further consequences.

There would be no indictment. Not only did the indictment not come on Wednesday, as had been leaked, it did not come on Friday because at 4 p.m. on Friday, December 18, 1998, the same day as the third affidavit was delivered, the attorney general's (AG) office pulled the plug on the grand jury, closed up their briefcases, and went home. That does not just happen. The AG knew there was a smart and determined force who would fight, and the sham case would be lost and could potentially dash his chances of being elected the next governor of Kentucky, as he had apparently hoped. For that reason, he also refused to talk to the media about his decision.

On the following Monday evening, I hastily called together a dinner at the Metropolitan Club atop Rivercenter to celebrate our victory of standing down the power-grabbers. In attendance were all the people who had assisted in our defense, as well as community supporters and several employees who had gone into the den of wolves to testify. Each attendee received a memento of the occasion that had inscribed in glass "Victory of Truth, Work, and Prayer." It is a fixture in many of our homes and offices that we take pride in.

However, I did make a mistake later. We had won the war, but the civil litigation with the county was still active. Obviously, the case against us financially had been seriously crippled by the grand jury dismissal. Yet people inside Corporex came to me. They were tired of this matter and did not want to continue diverting our energy and attention from growing the business, so we settled by giving the county a partial payment. It was enough to close out the case and as part of the settlement agreement, the county government and the county attorney declared on the record and admitted in writing that Corporex did no wrong in the bidding and that the responsibility for the entire mess belonged at the feet of the county government.

It was for us an exoneration, but it had taken 18 months of my life, because that is all I could think about or spend my time and energy on until we stood down the devious culprits. I was actually a registered Democrat at the time. Most of us in Kentucky were the old conservative-styled Democrat, that is when there was such a breed. Later, as a Democrat, I worked for the Republican who soundly and profoundly defeated the attorney general when he did in fact run for governor. I led a group of 16 leaders in our district evenly split between Democrats and Republicans and we were successful in bringing the entire state votes for my candidate up by 2.2 percent. We won the district by 37 percent. Some years later I switched my hat.

At the end of our celebratory dinner, Jerry Teller, an astute Cincinnati attorney and close counselor, approached me. "I'll bet you learned one thing from this," he said. "What?" I asked. "That there are a whole lot of people in jail who never did anything wrong."

Since then, I have made it known that I would pay to assist the defense of an innocent person unjustly accused.

And another profound piece of advice came from my special friend, the Honorable Nathaniel Jones. Nate Jones was a judge on the Sixth Circuit Federal Court of Appeals, but also a member of the board of governors of the Metropolitan Club. He was born in Youngstown, Ohio, and I had the privilege of attending the dedication of the new Federal Court House in Youngstown which was named for Judge Jones, and giving an invocation. I also served with him on the Underground Railroad Freedom Center project, and on the Marvin Lewis Community Fund. The Judge, as I often called him, at my 60th birthday stag party gave me a gift. In one of his eloquent speeches, he ended with, "You may be a white man, but you are my brother. You's the man." Whenever he introduced me to his friends of color he would add, "He is a brother," and they would take note, perk up, and acknowledge me again. And I feel the same about brother Nate.

The entire painful experience surrounding the ruthlessness of the perpetrators of the "Kenton County Bidding Scandal," as the media labelled it, along with the realization that a sham grand jury itself could even happen in America, and the fight itself was affecting me emotionally. Then one day I encountered Judge Jones in the lobby of the Metropolitan Club building and shared with him my latent feelings and resentments over this whole Kenton County Bidding Scandal and grand jury episode, even though it now appeared to be behind us. A traumatic experience like the threat of a felony indictment is not easily forgotten or put aside. One has to live such an attack on his reputation and character to fully appreciate the impact. I shared my feelings with the Judge, as a friend, and wondered what he thought.

Judge Jones was an astute man 20 years my senior and a personal friend of the late Nelson Mandela. Judge Jones had actually helped write the constitution of South Africa following the Apartheid era, and without much hesitation replied, "I am reminded of Nelson Mandela. After almost 30 years of unjustified imprisonment on Robben Island, when finally released, he went forward without losing a beat, as though the whole experience had not happened."

Nelson Mandela forgave and continued in his path of service to the people of South Africa. I got the message and think I have done a reasonable job of trying to take Mr. Mandela's approach, albeit in honesty there is still a bruise. Nelson Mandela was put away on a trumped-up charge as a terrorist. Though certainly not the same level of tragedy as Mr. Mandela's, I was accused in so many words of collusion, which was a stabbing charge for a man whose life was founded out of idealism, including not in the least, integrity.

The second half of the 1990s, the period following the credit crunch, was also a period of renewed and robust growth for Corporex once again. When I look back over our corporate history, the deep recessionary periods and their impacts are obvious. These are the times most remembered because they are most felt. The better times for some reason do not seem to have a matching emotional effect.

During that time, we had new development and construction projects simultaneously underway in Covington, Chicago, Indianapolis, Cleveland, Boston, Valley Forge, Baltimore, Washington, D.C.,, Illinois, and even Kansas City. These were larger hotels, multiple Five Seasons Sports Country Clubs units, office towers, distribution and manufacturing centers, too. Some of the larger investments were in Covington. At that time, we were the builders and general contractors for all of our own projects as well as for other clients, like Promus, Sherwin-Williams, International Paper, and others. We initiated more than $500 million worth of buildings during that period, including the second Tower of Rivercenter, plus the Marriott Hotel in Covington and Madison Place office building.

Chapter 12

Stepping Upward into the New Millennium

I have for a long time been mindful of what happened to shape a major U.S. city at the hands of only one man. What then can a corporation do that is even greater?

Daniel Burnham was the architect who, sometime after the big Chicago fire of 1871, developed master plans for Chicago. The plans, I was told, included preserving the new frontage along Lakeshore Drive; and then declaring that no buildings would be built on that land next to the water. He is, in my thinking, the major cause of the symbolic and iconic perspective we all have when we think of Chicago. We envision the high buildings, we see mostly the roadway, the water, and the parks along the water. I attribute that iconic vision to Daniel Burnham. And he wrote a statement that lives on today, and which we use at Corporex often in motivating situations, especially when addressing young people who are aspiring to their future. Burnham wrote:

> "Make no little plans; they have no magic to stir men's blood and probably themselves will not be realized. Make big plans; aim high in hope and work, remembering that a noble, logical diagram once recorded will never die."

Needless to say, we at Corporex took his direction to make big plans, and to aim high to heart. It was a busy time indeed, and probably when compared to the decade of the 1980s growth spurt, the years beginning with 2000 were a similar period of growth both in scope and moreover in dimension even larger. We came into the Millennium years with a head of steam. We were now taking bigger bites, larger buildings and larger investments, in more cities. The United States, not just the region, was where we felt comfortable. Geography no longer was an inhibitor; distance was made short via aircraft, and other markets had more energy. We would not be Corporex of today if we had not spread our wings nationally, and this helped to bridge recessions and frankly to make profit in hotter markets that could not be achieved in our hometowns. We started the new century with optimism, backed by a series of new, exciting projects. On top of the Madison Place Office building, we designed a setback to create a terrace in the sky, and four levels of very large condominiums which turned out very successful and became the catalyst for a new 25-story world-class condominium development to come later, called the Ascent.

Domaine de la Rive is the name of the unique structure on top of the office building. This is French for "Estate on the Riverbank." This project my wife and partner, Sue, can claim as being the source of inspiration. We had conducted a design competition of local architects for both the Marriott Hotel and the Madison Place Office building together as one mixed use project. One architect, KZF, responded with a creative idea to build residential condominiums on top of it all. I had asked for an extended-stay hotel, but KZF took the idea further. I took their plans home to Sue, and asked her: "Do you think something like this would work in Covington?" It would have been extremely pioneering and risky. You have to know my wife to appreciate her response. Sue asked a dozen questions for 30 minutes or more, then she said while pointing her finger on one of the plans: "Put my name on this one!" Well, well, what a surprise. We lived in a beautiful old Federal style home on acreage in the suburbs. Big trees lined the drive and every day when I returned, I had a sense of pride—that feeling that "everyman's home is his castle." We liked our home, but if Sue liked this project even more, I was all for a move.

Now then, I am a morning person. I wake up early, and often, as I was tiptoeing out of the bedroom in the dark, I would hear my sweet spouse's voice ask, "Are you working on my new home today?" And that is when Domaine de la Rive became the most important project on the table. I had not planned it for us; I only wanted to get her opinion. But I ended up with a mission. We went forward without any feasibility study for the residential units and I actually added a floor but eliminated the hotel underneath. If it was to be, then it might as well be magnificent.

It took five years to secure an office tenant for the foundational structure below the condos, and the financing to get the entire project underway. I felt sure there was a chance Sue would have a true French château up there, with many rooms like Versailles, should no one purchase units. After all, nothing like this had ever happened in Covington, and on top of a high-rise office? But I can tell you, it is a cool place to live.

The design Is, in fact, symbolic of a château in the European theme. It took time but it worked. Barry Larkin, the now-retired Hall of Famer, had just re-signed with the Cincinnati Reds. He was the first buyer. Sue was the second, combining two units into one. Jim and Kathy Orr, John and Mary Ann Boorne, and Wayne and Fran Carlisle came soon thereafter. Many executives and their families have since acquired the other eight homes, which are considered the best in the metro area. They are immediately on the river, looking out at the Cincinnati skyline.

Domaine de la Rive's acceptance on the part of top executives and home buyers provided the courage to undertake the world-class project called the Ascent some seven years later. If we had not undertaken this high-risk project, there would not be the incredible Ascent Residences. And if we had not undertaken the Ascent residential development, we would not have embarked on the incredible $1 billion-plus Ovation! project.

The Turn of the Century, We Turned with It—Westward

The next decade took us in a whole new direction, again in more than one dimension. Demographics of population trends demonstrated that most of the growth in the United States would occur from Denver to the West Coast.

In 1995 I purchased a 70-acre ranchette in Steamboat Springs, Colorado. My family had taken up skiing, although I hadn't begun to learn until I was in my early 40s, but one visit to Vail was all I needed to fall in love with the Rocky Mountains. Over time we skied different mountains and I, always the entrepreneur, looked at various places. We had a number of friends who owned homes in Beaver Creek, and I even optioned two lots there in the bottom of the credit crunch for $300,000 each. But Sue said Beaver Creek was too glitzy, so we skied at Park City and Deer Valley, and I bought a lot on top of the mountain in Deer Valley. I really liked Deer Valley. But then we looked at Steamboat Springs and loved its homey feel. As Sue likes to say, "a real place with real people." We love the mountains, the skiing, the hiking, biking—you name it. We love the little church and have been involved parishioners for 26 years. But for the longest time I refused development opportunities because Kentucky Eagles Ranch was my retreat location, my escape. Well, I probably should have stayed true to that promise. However, I did get involved in a major development there in 2005, thinking I would try to be a passive investor only. It did not work out that way.

I found myself flying over Denver constantly in the late 1990s to today, and, well, it just did not make sense not to take a look at this fast-growing population center for investment. I hired a good man, Glen Sibley, with a good reputation and experience in development. I focused on the big newly opened Denver International Airport (DIA) surroundings. At the time the talk was the new airport was just too far out on the prairie. Surely hotels would be needed there at some point. At the same time period the Olympics were being planned in Salt Lake City. I had paid $550,000 for the second-home lot in Deer Valley, and I sold it for $1,450,000 using a 1031 tax-free exchange to acquire a hotel site on Tower Road by DIA. We broke ground on an Embassy Suites Hotel in

2002 and it turned out to be a great performing property, which we transferred later into the Eagle Hospitality REIT launched in 2004. This investment placed us firmly in the Denver market. That activity was followed not long thereafter by taking on a challenging project in the city center at the new contemporary art museum campus.

Making a Splash

George Thorn is the owner of Mile High Development Company. The name alone says something about George. One had to be a Denver resident a long time ago to own the top name in the Mile High City. George operated a lean developer business and is well connected and respected politically. He held the development opportunity rights to the sites that surrounded the Frederic C. Hamilton Denver Contemporary Art Museum expansion, designed by the world-renowned architect Daniel Libeskind. The Hamilton contemporary art museum building structure is a beautiful model of world-class architecture—extraordinary architecture, as such is called. And so are the other buildings he designed for the museum campus. The first such proposed development was the Museum Residences, 57 extraordinary condominiums Libeskind designed on a campus site owned by the city. George drove up to visit me in Steamboat Springs for a weekend to get acquainted, bringing four separate project opportunities in Denver under his arms. We skied, got to know and like each other, and I became intrigued by the challenges of the Museum Residences architecture. He had several quotes from various venture financiers to fund, but none of them allowed George to retain much ownership upside or to be compensated for the development services. Many financial investors simply do not appreciate the effort and time and money that is devoted up front by developers to get a project underway. But we do. And again, nearly all the investors and developers were scared of this project because of the nature of the design and the high construction costs it would entail.

But I studied the plan closely and felt we could get our arms around both the design and the building costs. Besides, Corporex needed to make a splash in

Denver, to become known, and where better could we do that than in cooperation with all the high-level community movers and shakers who served on the board of the art museum itself? So we cut a deal with George Thorn, Corporex would put up the cash, we agreed to recognize a generous imputed value for the work George had done to date to bring the project forward, George would handle the marketing, Corporex would take charge of the design and construction and financing, and we both set out to make it happen.

I did not know if the project would be profitable; the condominium units were so unusual, and the location was not prime at the time. But it turned out that we were able to push the pricing to a range 35 percent higher than what George had projected initially, and the partnership made money. Better, George and I have become long-term friends.

It was through George that we were introduced to the impressive Daniel Libeskind. He was the design architect for our project in partnership with a local architectural firm. Daniel Libeskind and his design were selected in competition for the rebuilding of the World Trade Center site in lower Manhattan, a huge commendation. One would expect that an individual with his worldwide reputation and flair for the exotic would be an eccentric, elitist, difficult personality. But not Daniel. I had the opportunity to introduce Daniel when we did the ground-breaking ceremony for the Museum Residences. It went like this: "I want to introduce a person—pause—but I must first warn you, when this person speaks, he does not come from the heart, does not come from the heart—loooong pause! When he speaks, he comes from the soul." Daniel Libeskind's family were Holocaust victims and survivors too. He likes to describe how when he came to America at only five years old, he remembers mostly cruising around the Statue of Liberty as their ship made its way to Ellis Island. Daniel Libeskind has the unique ability to weave physical structures, environmental factors, human elements, and spiritual messages into his designs, and so does he endeavor in each case.

The Ascent, which he designed and which we developed in Covington, does just that, picking up on the Roebling bridge, the roof slopes follow the cables, the color blue, and the slope reaches for the heavens. We, too, have become good friends.

So, yes, we did make money on the Museum Residences, and we met another man in the process named Lanny Martin. Lanny is a very successful gentleman as well, chairman of a large private equity firm and also chairman of the Denver Art Museum board and others around Denver. We became partners later on to develop the *numero uno* hotel in Colorado, called the ART. The ART is truly a special hotel, very contemporary in design. It is also located at the museum center and filled with outstanding contemporary art, which Lanny curated and, in some cases, loaned. He is also a partner with us in the Hyatt Regency Aurora-Denver Conference Center and Hotel at the Anschutz Medical Campus in Aurora, Colorado. Both are properties we currently own and operate together.

I think our whole mindset has grown and evolved since we undertook such challenging projects as the Museum Residences in Denver and the Ascent back home. to once again think bigger and aim higher. This has raised us to an entirely different strata that separates us from our peers. In short, since that time, we have developed three separate world-class projects and are now bringing forward the fourth, Ovation!

Deciding to undertake a number of projects involving world-class architecture took us into a new mindset for what we developed, focusing on just two marketplaces: Denver and Greater Cincinnati, in particular the Northern Kentucky sector. This allowed us to maximize our available resources and people, and to take a hotel company public and sell it a short time later (I'll tell you more about Eagle Hospitality in a moment) in order to cope with the difficult period called the Great Recession that was to follow in 2009. In general, our projects got bigger in dollars and more upscale in nature. There is an excitement inherent in developing buildings of "world class" architecture, and that emotion is further enhanced when overlaying the tangible long-term impact such investments will have on the community it serves.

Remaking the Company Again

However, the turn of the century was another significant turning point for Corporex. Spread out as we were, building in far-off places, we were experiencing what I referred to as "cracks in the dike," which was something I had observed happening too often in construction companies that got large. The fees considered to be market rate for construction services had been compressed like every other business in the 35-year period since our founding. We could buy construction services for 3-4 percent times cost, and three fourths of our construction volume was billings for our own development project accounts. We were taking money from one pocket and putting it in the other. We began to wonder if it was even possible to be as efficient in, say, Washington, D.C. (where we were building a hotel) as a local contracting firm domiciled in that community. So we made a major call, decided to exit the construction business, and to hire other general contractors to build our buildings, too. This was an especially tough call since construction had been our original core business. It was where we began and what led us into the real estate development and investing field. But I thought it was the right thing to do.

Reducing our staffing by nearly 100 people was at stake and so I tried to sell, or give, our construction company and its backlog worth nearly $90 million at the time, to another firm. There were only a few that might qualify, but not really, because of our design-build approach. So we began to award third-party contracts for new work while slowly working off the backlog. The last project was a large Embassy Suites hotel in Cleveland, completed in mid-2001.

What was really behind this decision was the thought that it would be better to re-direct top management focus that had to be given to an intensive construction process, managing many people, to focusing more energy on our investment portfolio, the development projects and assets. By doing this we would be ahead of the game. It turned out to be a smart decision for many reasons, as time went forward.

Eagle Hospitality, a Publicly Traded Company

In April 2004 Corporex successfully raised $165 million on the New York stock exchange to fund a new company, Eagle Hospitality Property Trust. We seeded the company with nine full-service hotel properties we had developed. They included the Marriott, an Embassy Suites, and a Hilton in Kentucky, and a series of Embassy Suites in Tampa, Cleveland, Columbus, and Denver, plus a Hyatt Regency tower in downtown Rochester, New York, and another Marriott in Chicago. Bill Blackham, who was an officer of Corporex in finance, became the full-time CEO of Eagle. I put together an impressive board of directors, mostly from larger publicly traded companies, and we undertook to selectively acquire a series of individual hotels in Boston, Puerto Rico, Los Angeles, and Phoenix, nearly doubling the EBITDA over three years. Although our stock remained at the same price as when we launched, $9.75 per share, 2005, 2006, and 2007 were good times in the economy and real estate was fetching strong sale prices.

To deal with a difficult issue in 2007, we held a special board session and identified several options, one of which was a loosely offered idea to sell the entire company after only three years in business. I was chairman of the board, and Corporex plus a close group of investors owned 24 percent of Eagle, essentially the controlling votes. The other directors looked at me, knowing that I would not consider such a crazy notion. I thought for a moment and surprised them with my response: "We are in a really hot real estate market environment. Properties are selling at very high prices, and if we are truly representing the best interests of our shareholders, which is our duty, we owe it to them and ourselves to take a look." No one thought that I would really give up the company, because that would involve paying a lot of deferred taxes, for which our partners and I would all be obligated. And Commonwealth Hotels, our affiliate, would lose the contracts on managing the portfolio of hotels. Entrepreneurs just do not sell, and there were multiple ways Eagle could be beneficial to Corporex in the future. Giving up the management contract revenue was a big consideration, but as a fiduciary for the shareholders, I could not allow myself to be swayed by that.

Well, this entrepreneur was willing to consider a sale. Being novice to the public markets, what I did not know is that "taking a look" in the trade means you are going to sell the company: no turning around likely. Morgan Stanley was hired to broker the deal, there were at least five sound bids, and we closed on August 15th, 2007, for $13.35 per share—a 43 percent premium over market. Genius.

It turns out that 60 days later, the deal would never have closed. Our stock would have dropped in value to less than $2 just six months later. We know this for fact. That is what happened to peer companies of the same type when the financial markets began to collapse shortly thereafter in 2008. But this sale also put a big slug of cash in our Corporex coffers heading into the big looming financial meltdown. Once again, our timing, due to our principled nature to do the right thing for our shareholders rather than self, carried the day.

People have suggested that being chairman of a public company must have been frustrating for an entrepreneur like me, but I did not have that sense. We have always operated Corporex as though in many ways it were a public company with full accountability to shareholders, even though I am the sole shareholder. For this reason, we have a very strong board of directors and we pay them for their roles. Not only are they equipped to deal with the needs should I die or be killed, but I wanted them there as a matter of self-discipline. I respect my board members; they are all successful people of their own making, and have good business as well as personal principles. I would have no problem leading another publicly traded enterprise, as it just did not feel any different.

Fitzsimons Village

During the financial meltdown of 2008, a large commercial mixed-use development in early stages located east of Denver proper came to our attention. The property was directly across the highway from the big new Anschutz Medical Campus and the local developers were in financial distress. These developers had been negotiating with Children's Hospital to build and lease a multistory office building on a small piece of their 32-acre mixed use site called Fitzsimons Village. This building was to house their entire administration staffing for the new hospital Children's was completing just across the highway. For a lot of reasons, but mostly due to the pain of the recession and considerable short-term debt, they lost the ability to pay the bank lenders, were in default on a large underlying land mortgage loan, and they simply could not pull it together nor deliver the building to the hospital tenant. We stepped in, acquired their interests in the entire development both the 32 acres and this building opportunity, and negotiated with the banks who held the loan. In doing so, we also added our credit and our credibility to the project, and that made the banks comfortable during a very challenging economic year not only for developers but for the financial banking industry as well, and this allowed the initial developers to be freed of heavy obligations.

We completely redesigned the office building in-house over a fourth of July weekend using our architects, we negotiated the lease to signature, and secured the financing when no one was getting such loans. Financing the buildings was, in retrospect, the easier task, although in 2009 and 2010 at the bottom of the recession, nothing was easy when it came to money. Financing the essential infrastructure improvements was nearly impossible then. Almost every new project in the United States was stalled, but because we had sold our stock in Eagle Hospitality, we were financially prepared at a critical time.

It was necessary not only to secure financing for the office and hotel, but we needed an additional $17 million for construction of the Fitzsimons Village grand entrance, for reconstruction of the highway median, and for adding turn lanes and signaling. Moreover, we had to design and construct a very long connector bridge into the medical campus, spanning the entire six-lane highway. Industrial revenue bonds (IRBs) were commonly used to pay for such infrastructure improvements, but IRBs at the time had not been marketable for at least two years. Fortunately, we succeeded when others did not.

At a dinner one evening just before the bonds were issued, Sam Sharp of Davidson and Company in Denver told the following story: "My firm has not been able to find buyers for a bond of this nature for more than two entire years, but this loan is going to happen for one reason only—because it's Corporex." He continued, "Apparently, you had a large bond on a high-rise residential project in Cincinnati (the Ascent), and the holders of those bonds thought for sure they had a problem and that you would default. But you stepped up and paid off the balance. Oppenheimer was one of the larger owners of those bonds and Oppenheimer is leading this new issue as a result of their experience with your company."

Well, imagine how good we felt that we had stood up, once again, and done the right thing—and again we were rewarded. The bondholders had cause for concern because our bonds on the Ascent were backed by a $67 million letter of credit issued by Wachovia Bank, one of the biggest in the country at the time. Wachovia, along with other banks, was suffering during the financial meltdown. Indeed, we were having trouble getting the bond holders to renew and extend their debt every 30 days due to Wachovia's problems, and interest rates were rising quickly on our Ascent bonds as a result. We had the money in the bank, we believed in the property and ourselves, and we stepped up—and again that made the difference.

But this story also sheds light on the devastating state of affairs in the financial markets in 2009, 2010, and 2011. We had ignition due to our creativity, our discipline, our balance sheet, and our commitment and proceeded to break ground in the bottom-most part of that recession for Children's Hospital's administration building, a seven-story structure together with a large parking garage. Moreover, we simultaneously broke ground on a Spring Hill Suites Marriott hotel next door to the office building. As part of the deal with Children's Hospital, we designed and constructed a connector bridge from our development site to the big medical campus which spans a six-lane roadway. We did something novel by building the bridge on the side of the roadway. We secured a special permit and closed the highway to traffic on a Friday night beginning at 10 p.m. to lift and swing this 150-ton structure on top of the concrete pedestals we also constructed. I could not be present that night in person, but four cameras were installed so that I could see and guide the hoisting from all sides on my computer screen 1,000 miles away. I watched with the phone open talking to our local managers until 4 a.m. on Saturday when the structure was lowered over the anchor bolts. Then I went to bed. That was fun.

The Fitzsimons Village development was incredibly well-timed for us. Corporex was able to source a total of $725 million in the very depths of that crash when lenders were running for cover, break ground when most projects came to a screeching halt, and make money on those developments.

At the opening event for the Springhill Suites Hotel, officers of Children's Hospital suggested they wanted a four-star hotel in which to put their guests; the Spring Hill would not be high-end enough for them. So we came up with an idea. This local marketplace in itself would not support the costs of such an upscale hotel; but if the City of Aurora would build the conferencing center, we would build the hotel on the Fitzsimons Village development integrated with the conferencing center. The idea took hold and the city responded energetically. To accomplish this, we formed a venture where the city did, in fact, float $30 million in bonds, pay for the conference center plus a 600-car parking structure, and we built the first-class Hyatt Regency above it. This has proven a catalytic project for the fast-growing city of Aurora, as well as for the remainder of our property.

Commonwealth Hotels, our hotel management company, manages both the hotel and conferencing center together. This was a true public-private partnership. Currently two separate national apartment developers are underway to build nearly 700 living units on property in Fitzsimons Village, which we sold them, and we have plans for a ten-story office building underway. The Fitzsimons Village project turned out to be a big financial contributor to our firm. Denver as a whole has been good to us, the business community welcomed us with open arms, and it is a city on the move; today it seems everyone wants to live there.

In reality, Colorado has been good to us ever since we first engaged corporately there 20 years ago.

Alpine Mountain Ranch and Club

I mentioned that in 2005 we invested in a 1,200-acre parcel of land on the outskirts of Steamboat Springs, tucked up under the ski mountain. An entrepreneurial gentleman from Denver, the late Warren Sheridan, and his partners, all about his age, had assembled more than 45 small parcels of land to build a second ski base location with housing. Calling it Alpine Mountain Ranch, it was to Warren a passion project similar to my own in Northern Kentucky. He had worked on it for at least 25 years, but failed to get the concept implemented. But what a beautiful piece of land it was and is.

Another passionate man named Andy Daly was, and is, widely known in the ski industry. Shortly before I met him, Andy was the president of Vail Ski Resorts at the time when Apollo Global out of New York City acquired the company. In the process, Andy was replaced and was left looking for opportunities to develop real estate. People view Vail Resorts as a ski business, but actually it is a major real estate developer in mountain resorts. I had passed on multiple good opportunities in Steamboat Springs, because it was my place to go to escape, but this land was special and again, as with Dan Fay and Kevin Moloney, Andy seemed like a good guy to partner with. I like partnerships, I get energy from a partnership when it works, and I think, well I know, I am a good partner-type as well.

The key to this property again took creativity, and much more—water. Whenever developing or building in Colorado, water and sun are two resources that are essential. This property had no domestic water access. A man named Don Valentine, who I knew from my relations in Steamboat, had some time ago incorporated a quasi-private/public water company on the property next door, designing the equipment with an eye to this 1,200-acre parcel of land.

I met with Don over my kitchen table at Kentucky Eagle's Ranch and we cut a deal for us to buy his water company. I remember we wrote the contract long-hand on a legal pad at the time and signed it. Without his water company—securing water would require a new water plant, involving lots of governmental permitting or alternatively accessing a river which is 1 mile away from the site, and this was not feasible. With the water issue resolved, Andy and Corporex could move forward where no one else could. Warren had painstakingly assembled the 1,200 acres over many years, and he was emotionally attached to the property and just could not get himself to sell, but his partners had grown inpatient. We came up with another idea. We offered him 5 percent continuing ownership in our whole development so that he could keep an emotional attachment, and that made the deal.

Given our investment simultaneously at the Museum Residences, and now this 1,200-acre residential development, well we were now squarely entrenched in the residential development field I had avoided for 40 years.

We all agreed that Andy would be the operating partner, and my intention was for Corporex to be a passive investor, if possible. That way, I wouldn't have to be involved in the day-to-day management of the project and could still enjoy my escape-from-work environment, as I had always thought of Steamboat.

Alpine Mountain Ranch was the name Warren Sheridan had always used for the property, and the local community knew it by that name, so we kept it. We were one of the very first developers to undertake a new land planning system (LPS), which the county government had adopted. In essence, under this new LPS policy, for every 100 acres we agreed to place in preservation status, never to be further developed, the county would allow one additional five-acre lot for sale. In our case, that increased the developable sites from 34 to 43 and, at the same time, created a wildlife preserve. The property is home to large herds of elk, and there is even a family of moose. Being contiguous with the national forest, there are also bear, fox, and some cats, which one does not see much of. It is an incredible 1,200 acres and the homesites are situated to take advantage of the views of the Flattop Mountain range and the sun. Views and the sun, and water source are the key elements for a good investment in the Rocky Mountains. It is not wise to invest if those items are not inherent to the site.

Early in the development process, while we were still putting infrastructure in place, Andy and I and a few others flew up to the Yellowstone Club in Montana to visit and inspect their very popular, and somewhat similar, development. Yellowstone Club has become the scene for the billionaires; it seems that all of them, beginning with Bill Gates, must have homes there. We came home with one big takeaway: we were underestimating the values inherent in our own development. When we compared our site and plan's attributes to that of the Yellowstone Club, we upgraded our thinking.

On the way home, we decided to rename the project "Alpine Mountain Ranch and Club," and to add club amenities, to raise our sights in all respects. We designed two guest cabins and another building that could potentially be a combination swimming pool, fitness, spa space, and more. We designed a magnificent main entrance with walls and a gated arrival. These components were added to the lodge and equestrian center and "the Boss's Hermitage," which is a cute one-room building with a fireplace, bunk, and monk's desk, all buried in the woods and accessible only by foot or horse. It was a fun idea and well received by everyone.

The planning approval process in the Colorado mountains is difficult and protracted. We took title in early 2005 but could not begin infrastructure improvements involving six miles of roadway, six miles of water extensions, electrical, etc., until the second half of 2007. We completed the work just in time for the financial meltdown of 2008–2009. We had presold only seven lots and then did not sell another lot for nearly 10 years. Talk about a problem! A $35 million development loan to service, another $16 million in cash equity invested, and no sales of lots—zero. What to do? Corporex owned 57 percent fully diluted, as there were some limited partners in addition to Andy Daly and Warren. Corporex was a co-guarantor on the loan and the biggest signatory. The lenders were looking to Corporex.

The financial meltdown of 2008–2009 was unprecedented. Once again, the project was frozen and there was nothing we could do to get sales. Often, when a developer is in this situation, especially in such crucial recessionary straits, he will default and cause the property to be foreclosed on. That is what happened to several other competing developments in Steamboat Springs, but this has never been Corporex's style if we could at all avoid it. However, neither Andy nor any of the others were in a position to fund such an unknown.

The Corporex relationship with US Bank, the lender, went back at least 20-plus years at the time, beginning with the Rivercenter loans in 1987. We have always valued long-term relationships. We made a deal with the bank to, in effect, buy their loan position at full par value, not asking for relief, and over a period of five years unilaterally repaid this land loan on behalf of the partnership. It was appropriate that we step up in this way as general partners: Corporex and Andy were 80/20, so it was the right thing to do. We advanced what were for us huge amounts of operating money to the partnership to make these payments to US Bank, and subsequently to keep staff employed on the site and to protect the name and reputation of the first-class project. We had a stated goal: "To come out the other end of the recession with the number one reputation in the local community for the project, untainted by financial restructuring." That has worked, but it sure took a long time; we had no idea the recession for such real estate would last more than eight years. I had assumed it would be the usual two to three years.

Would we have done it differently, cut bait so to speak, if we knew the amount of money this project would consume or that we would have to be patient for such a long duration? I doubt it. Corporex has always been a long-term player, believing in what we invest in or undertake, living up to its commitments and obligations. But had we been able to invest those sums into the stock markets alongside of other funds during the recovery, the financial outcome would be four times greater. So be it.

Alpine Mountain Ranch and Club is today the premier place to invest in all of Routt County, Colorado, where Steamboat Springs is located. Steamboat Springs is a community of 14,000 people, growing in prominence and prestige in great part due to the contribution Alpine Mountain Ranch and Club has made.

But during those trying times, not only did we service the debt, in essence becoming the lender, but we also made another bold move in 2010, near the very bottom of the recession. Part of our land planning permit included a special agreement with the county government that if we acquired another, less valuable parcel of land in the pristine Yampa River Valley below the development, and commit that parcel to conservation, the county would allow 20 more lots to be located on our mountainside site. We had no idea if we would ever be able to take advantage of this option.

In the depths of the Great Recession from 2010 to 2011, lots of people were financially stressed, not least Corporex, especially since we were now servicing both the major urban site we had bought for Ovation! in Kentucky and the Alpine Mountain Ranch and Club burden. But in that same period, another opportunity came to our attention. The Steamboat Springs airport is named after a fellow named Bob Adams, an entrepreneur who initially founded the ski hill as well. His family owned a 3,000-acre parcel, though it was not part of the conservation parcel the county had incentivized us with. But John Adams was able to get the county commission to qualify his land for that purpose. We made a deal.

We did not buy the land outright, we simply agreed to pay the land owner $7.5 million to place a restrictive covenant on 900 acres to permanently preserve it, so that it could not be developed. They could still use the land for agricultural purposes without violating the covenant. Having another twenty sites to sell was in my mind the only way this project could turn profitable, given the cost to carry the debt and operating burden through the recession. It was a bold move once again with an eye toward long-term success. And again, the move appears to be successful long term, as we sold the first of those 20 homesites just recently for $3.5 million. Consider the return on that investment if we can repeat such sales within a reasonable period of time. This one courageous act undertaken during the worst of times is what may allow us and our partners to eventually recover their investments.

In 2017 I decided that nine years was long enough to sit on this fully developed land asset without sales. We needed to take definitive action. My sense was that the markets were coming back and that we needed to publicly relaunch the Alpine Mountain Ranch and Club project and to claim our success in weathering the storm. We needed to create energy where there had not been for all those years. This meant we would be going in even deeper. We committed to building not one, but three speculative market homes ranging in size from 5,000 to 6,000 sq. ft. each, with five bedrooms and mountain contemporary designs. The public's preferred aesthetic was changing from traditional heavy-beam mountain construction to the new world of contemporary home design.

But then in 2020 came the pandemic and, simultaneously, street riots sprang up throughout the country in places where such demonstrations were unheard of. The public was scared and looking to move to safer terrain. Steamboat turned out to be a desirable spot. In July 2020 we sold a lot for $1.45 million, then another shortly thereafter for $1.8 million, then one for $1.85 million, and then more until we had achieved six sales in just six months, the last being for just over $2 million. But it did not stop there. In 2021, Alpine Mountain Ranch and Club sold 17 lots to prospective homeowners with prices that rose to $3 million before year-end. Since then, sales have reached values of $3.5 million for lots in a new section called Upland Preserve.

In order to close these sales, we had to make another bold move. Our buyers were sometimes reluctant to commit because the pandemic had made it difficult to find builders to build the homes. That and shortages of materials presented a huge hurdle. My solution was to create a design and construction business unit.

I personally spent three months to recruit and staff Alpine Master Builders, a full-service design and construction subsidiary. Now we could promise to build if a person bought a lot. In short order, we had nine homes in the works. For the first time, Corporex was in the custom home building business, but building unique, large second homes ranging from $4.7 to $6.5 million each. We currently have one under construction that will approach $10 million in construction value. Fifteen homes are under construction in the development simultaneously as I share this story.

Alpine Mountain Ranch and Club is a testament to strength inherent in high-quality development, long-term perspective, perseverance, and commitment.

The Ascent—Returning Home

Back home we were busy as well. Our experience with the Museum Residences and Daniel Libeskind's world-class architecture had given me some ideas about a building on the one last site we owned in the Rivercenter development. This site had views of the river and Cincinnati skyline, and condominium developments were very much in vogue during the first half of the new decade. We had just completed the pre-sales process at Museum Residences, which was a huge success, and had learned from that and also our success at Domaine de la Rive in Covington that we could likely interest enough buyers to relocate to a very high-touch building. While condos were hot, office buildings were not and investing in them was not justified, but this seemed a good bet.

I tried to get three local architects to draw a "special building." I used the phrase "something which twists into the sky" to describe it, to try and inspire a new world-class concept. Three local architects competed with their concepts, none of which matched the vision in my mind. I picked up the phone and called famed architect Daniel Libeskind, whom I had just met in Denver, suspecting that this building might be too small for him to entertain, but also starting to wonder if only someone of his caliber could help me capture my idea.

He said, "I will be right down," and he and Nina, his wife and business partner, were there within 10 days.

I gave him the same pitch I gave the other architects, trying to describe the nature of the building I wanted to design. He said, "Give me six weeks and $50,000 and I will come up with a solution."

Well, we had never done something like that before—pay someone in advance—and that was a lot of money for a schematic, but it turned out to be well worth the leap. Exactly six weeks later, a team of ours visited his New York offices overlooking the Ground Zero site in lower Manhattan. He had a design and a plastic model, and drawings posted on the walls of a small room.

After studying it briefly, I asked everyone to leave the room so I could just sit at the table and study this exotic building. I decided it was not so extreme and if we built it with concrete, we could form the shapes.

I left the room with this statement: "I think we can build it, and if we can, we will."

The project did not then have a name yet. We selected "The Ascent" based on a competition we gave to the team of architects midway through the design process. When one looks at the building shape and the perfectly matched name, they never forget the Ascent.

The Ascent and the Museum Residences both won international design awards. Usually, such extraordinary designs are affordable only to public or not-for-profit owners. To the best of our knowledge, these two projects are the only world-class-designed buildings funded by a private developer in the United States, and we are very proud that they are.

The Banks, a Development in Cincinnati

In 1991 the City of Cincinnati and Hamilton County together had adopted a comprehensive development plan for a project to be known as the Banks, which was to be located on the riverbank on the Ohio side. However, as of 2005, 14 years later, little progress had been made moving the plan forward.

The Banks project had been discussed with various developers for many years to no avail. It was a hard sell to people outside the area. It appeared the Cincinnati community and politicos just could not get their act together. However, during that same period Corporex had undertaken the Rivercenter project on the south riverbanks in Kentucky, and constructed five high-rise buildings.

The *Cincinnati Enquirer* had long employed a Pulitzer Prize–winning cartoonist named Jim Borgman, who on more than one occasion used Corporex's development progress at Rivercenter in Northern Kentucky to criticize the City of Cincinnati officials' inaction on the Banks project. The comparisons seemed to get under the skin of some of the old guard in Cincinnati and the politicians, who began to develop a negative view of Corporex and Bill Butler. Although Corporex had no involvement in the cartoons, resentment started to build on the other side of the river. One cartoon would have been fine, but Jim ended up drawing several that painted Cincinnatians in a somewhat negative light.

Of course, people at Corporex were buying up prints each time they were published. Jim even autographed the first one for me, signing it, "Bill, from one artist to another." On the other hand, Borgman's messages could have been suggesting Corporex should undertake the Banks project. Who knows?

After years of public procrastination on getting the Banks development underway, Corporex was eventually asked if we would be willing to pay $10 million to acquire the development rights—actually, the air rights—over a six-block area. Buying air rights over public parking structures is tantamount to owning the deed.

JIMBORGMAN
Welcome to NORTHERN KENTUCKY
NO, WAIT... LET'S BUILD THE STADIUM SIX INCHES TO THE LEFT.
OHIO
TO BILL, FROM ONE ARTIST TO ANOTHER... JIMBORGMAN

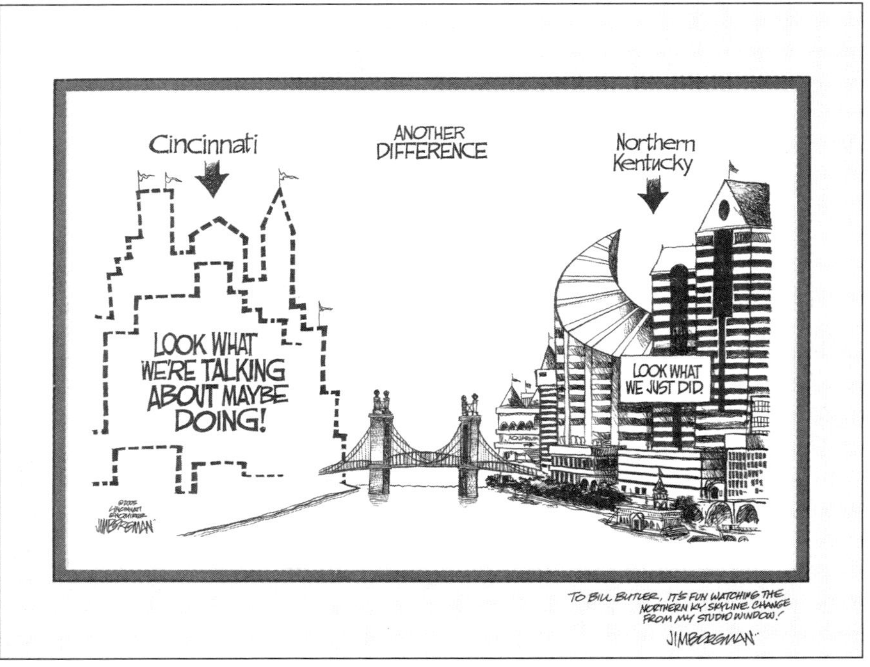
Cincinnati
ANOTHER DIFFERENCE
Northern Kentucky
LOOK WHAT WE'RE TALKING ABOUT MAYBE DOING!
LOOK WHAT WE JUST DID.
JIMBORGMAN
TO BILL BUTLER, IT'S FUN WATCHING THE NORTHERN KY SKYLINE CHANGE FROM MY STUDIO WINDOW!
JIMBORGMAN

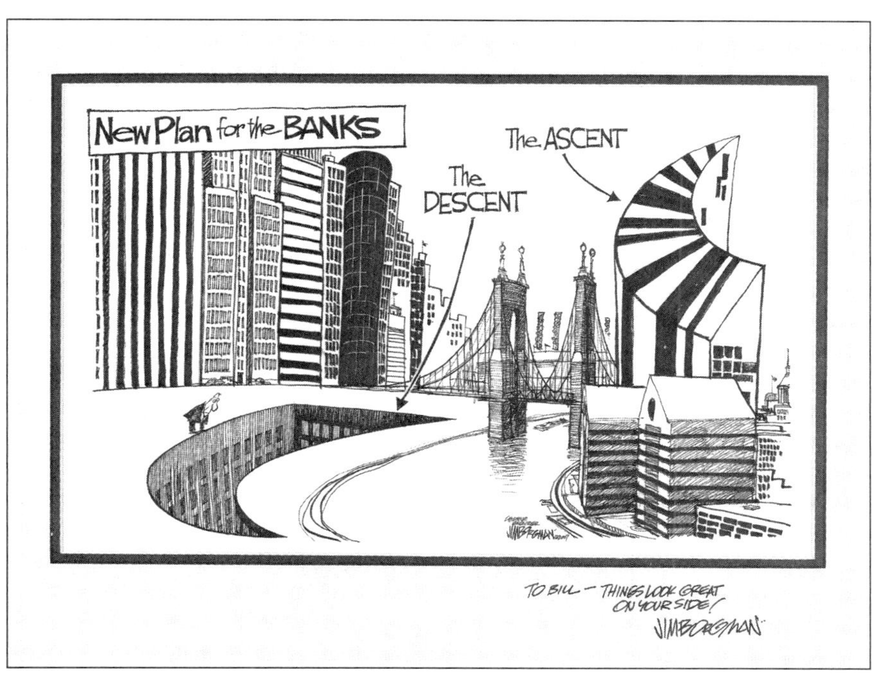
New Plan for the BANKS
The ASCENT
The DESCENT
TO BILL — THINGS LOOK GREAT ON YOUR SIDE!
JIM BORGMAN

JIM BORGMAN
THE BLANKS
NKY
HUFF! PUFF! WHEW! HUFF! PUFF!
Development Derby
TO BILL — AND THEY'RE OFF!
JIM BORGMAN

This was an interesting proposition, and we said yes without hesitation. We were excited to have the opportunity to make an impact on the Cincinnati skyline. After all, we in Northern Kentucky feel a part of Cincinnati. Corporex had investments there. We contributed to the arts and other charitable agencies. We were on boards. In fact, we had worked on the very first master plan for the entire five-parcel project. Jeanne Schroer, one of Corporex's officers at the time, devoted extensive time to the citizens committee assembled to develop the plan. She wrote the book.

Corporex also had been a significant donor to the National Underground Railroad Freedom Center, which is located in the exact center of the Banks project's footprint. In addition, I had served as a member of the building committee on construction and recognized the importance of this project. On top of that, I had a vision of its potential as an anchor—a centerpiece, so to speak—for the entire surrounding neighborhood. The Freedom Center's high-quality, unique architecture was a property into which the entire community had invested nearly $125 million. I envisioned an entire neighborhood of similar character with pedestrian-friendly streets, townhomes, street-level retail and entertainment, as well as office buildings and hotels—all in a coordinated, master-planned design and similar architectural features. Being a visionary, I had a picture in my mind of what could be.

My vision, if carried out, would create a wonderful iconic front-door project for Cincinnati's future—a new progressive look for the next 200 years. Maybe because we were on the other side of the river looking over at the skyline, we at Corporex saw something in Cincinnati that its political or business leaders did not recognize about themselves or their community. To me, this site should be the actual front door of the city, even though it faces south, toward the river and Northern Kentucky. In the old days, the "front door" to Cincinnati was from the north or northeast, in the direction of the capital in Ohio. But that was prior to the population and growth in Northern Kentucky and the airport being located in Kentucky. To me, the modern-day front door is oriented toward the south, as viewed from Kentucky. People approach the city from the south when coming from the international airport. The skyline of Cincinnati is an attractive scene as people come down the hill on Interstate 75 to the urban areas.

I had a picture painted in my mind of consistent architecture, stretching four blocks, both Eastward and Westward, on each side of the Freedom Center. It would be a derivative of the appearance and high-touch contemporary architecture of the Freedom Center. We felt that, if done correctly, the native Cincinnatians who could afford a high-quality home would relocate to this master-planned neighborhood. (We discovered later we were wrong.)

A letter of intent was signed to enter into exclusive negotiations with Hamilton County government because the county was leading the effort on behalf of both the city and county. The letter of intent stated that the parties would complete the final development agreement within six months. We were confident we could do it. A number of the leading CEOs in Cincinnati, in particular the very influential Carl Lindner Jr., chairman of American Financial Corporation; A. G. Lafley, who at the time was CEO of Procter & Gamble; and others, endorsed and supported Corporex's involvement. Many had witnessed what we had accomplished on the Kentucky shores. So we began in earnest to complete an exclusive development document similar to what we had previously developed with the City of Covington for Rivercenter.

All was well and progressing for about four months. The selection of Corporex had been announced by the two governments, and we were moving ahead. Then, after about the four-month mark, something changed. The meetings became unproductive and the kinds of questions being asked by Hamilton County's attorney for the Banks project, Tom Gabelman, just did not make sense; they were not material to the task at hand. We were not getting anything accomplished in work sessions on the document.

Coincidentally, these meetings turned peculiar the moment Corporex began conducting pre-sales presentations to a list of 200 preferred buyers for the Ascent high-rise we were moving to develop in Covington.

During pre-sales meetings with prospective buyers, we learned that the clientele we were targeting for living units in the Banks project was essentially the same as for the Ascent. One conclusion became obvious. This group, at this level of wealth, was not likely to relocate to Cincinnati proper due to their feelings about the city's governance and security and safety concerns related to rising crime levels in the urban core. This was around 2005–2007. The lion's share of these buyers were empty-nesters and retirees.

While this new information was a concern on the one hand, the negotiations had simultaneously stalled on the other. Something was seriously wrong, and Phil Heimlich, the top executive for Hamilton County, was not being forthcoming about the problem. In retrospect, I suspect either the building trades unions, certain competitive contractors, or a developer—with influence in Cincinnati—pressured Phil Heimlich to kill the deal.

I had witnessed this kind of competitive act back in the 1990s, when certain unidentified forces in Cincinnati gutted the Metropolitan Growth Alliance. If a negotiation does not get out of the gate on a good path, experience says that the road ahead will be dangerously bumpy. We did not have the time or patience to be reading about ourselves in conflicts with the public in the media regularly. We also knew that the City of Newport was preparing to auction approximately 15 acres of its former subsidized housing site for development. This parcel was in Kentucky but had stunning views of the Cincinnati skyline, and we had already proven the people with money would, in fact, choose to reside in Kentucky, in great part due to the lower crime rate.

So, not knowing if we would be the developer when that moved forward, Corporex announced it was terminating development negotiations with Hamilton County. Although we disappointed a number of business execs who had pushed for Corporex to develop the Banks—and frankly it disappoints me to this day—it was clearly the best course of action. There were strong forces at work behind the scenes preventing Corporex from being the Banks' developer, and we just did not need the hassle. We didn't want a fight, so we walked away. As expected, the Banks stalled again.

After a while, a new group of Cincinnati business executives and community leaders was organized to take over the process, to get the project moving forward. A developer out of Atlanta was given the development rights and built two market-driven quality-level apartment properties without consideration of the potential long-term benefit to Cincinnati's skyline. The county and city have so far spent more than $110 million to install only 60 percent of the parking garages that Corporex had committed to build for $57 million as part of the deal. Instead, the city and county will have spent an estimated in the end $150 million to get an equal amount of parking and deck constructed.

Only three buildings have been developed around the Banks in 16 years since we walked away, and these properties look nothing like the Freedom Center, nor are they of the same quality. Two are apartment projects that do not resemble even each other; one is a glass office building with no compatible design to the apartment buildings. And where Corporex had agreed to write a check for $10 million up front for the air lots, the sites were transferred to out-of-town developers without such consideration.

Lesson: If you want a high-quality outcome, choose a developer that cares, one with a vested interest in doing something for its community. If you want the development to make a big contribution to the community, begin with a vision—and stick with it. It is obvious that there is no overarching vision for the Banks any longer.

We paid a big price to acquire the site in Newport but again closed immediately before the 2008–2009 financial meltdown and the Great Recession that followed. That delayed our ability to move forward for nearly 10 years, but we are currently underway with a $1 billion development that will paint a beautiful picture and make a big difference in the future of Northern Kentucky, but will also add character to the entire urban core, including Cincinnati.

I drive by the site of the Banks development frequently and still have my vision of what could have been I think to myself, "What a missed opportunity." Our plan would have changed the entire perception of Cincinnati as a place, would have elevated it with a new face—a new image for the mind. Neither those who worked so diligently to prevent our involvement nor the public at large will ever understand how beautiful and iconic it could have been.

Chapter 13

For Every Problem, an Opportunity

The next serious recession for us came along in 2008—what became known as the "Great Recession," to relate its scale to the Great Depression of the 1930s. People on Wall Street spoke about a meltdown in financial terms during the earliest months of this debacle. The contraction lasted for nearly eight years, at least in our business. I did not expect that and even held a forum in Steamboat Springs to express our bullishness on a two- to three-year recovery based on historical charts. But no, this one caused a slog effect, yet we were probably more prepared corporately to weather this downturn, as we had just sold Eagle Hospitality, a major holding, and received significant cash. People, mostly younger bankers, would ask me during this downturn, "This is the worst you have ever seen, right?" and I would just shake my head—no, not even close.

Those young people who asked that question had not lived or been working in the banking and financial or the real estate development sectors in the early 1990s. That was when the real estate credit crunch occurred. The credit crunch was limited mostly to our field of business, commercial development. Even housing development moved forward in the credit crunch uninterrupted and could access loans. Other industries were able to move forward while commercial developers were failing everywhere in the country.

Again, as in 1989 leading into the credit crunch, we had sold a portfolio of properties to Equitable Life. We acted early once again. In late 2007 we took visionary action and sold Eagle Hospitality Property Trust. In retrospect, our timing appears genius, but truthfully, it was just the outcome of doing the right thing for the right reasons in both cases.

The ART, a Hotel

The Great Recession that began in 2008 and lasted until 2016 did, in fact, set the company back by holding up major endeavors. It put Ovation! on hold for 10 years, and Alpine Mountain Ranch and Club in the mountains for an equal span. These were our two largest projects planned at the beginning of this period.

That same meltdown delayed our development plans in Denver at the Art Museum, as well. We owned, as part of the original joint venture with Mile High Development, another site on Broadway Street and had in mind building a hotel soon after the completion of the Museum Residences. While private development was frozen for years during the Great Recession, governmental agencies went forward, including a new and very large justice center on the opposite corner from our site. This reinforced the concept for our proposed hotel, which we had long ago decided to name the ART.

We invited one of Denver's community leaders to invest, and he suggested that he would subscribe to the entire issue. Rather than having a typical general/limited partnership with many investors, we moved forward in a true joint-venture relationship with Mr. Lanny Martin of Platte River Equity.

We both wanted the ART Hotel to be a four-star, high-touch contemporary boutique product. Lanny is the chairman of the board of the Denver Art Museum, itself and an astute collector of postwar contemporary art. We did a written agreement, but we also had a handshake deal. I said I would take care of the building design and construction and he would direct, choose, and acquire the artwork, and that is exactly what we did.

Office Buildings

First Office Building—1965
Covington, KY

First Turn-Key Construction Job—1970

Erlanger Crescent Springs Industrial Park—1970

New Headquarters Building—1971
Erlanger/Crescent Springs Industrial Park

First Speculative Office Building—1971

Ole Brickyard Park—Mid-1970's

Florence Space Center—1981-82

First Multi-Story Office Building
Lookout Corporate Center—1982

President's Plaza—Tampa, FL 1984

Commonwealth
Hilton Hotel—First Hotel
(Mid-1980's)

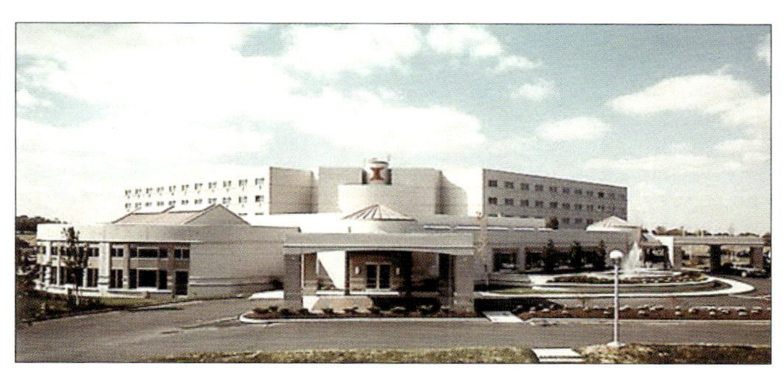

Corporex Plaza—Tampa, FL (Mid-1980's)

Crystal Terrace—Nashville, TN (Mid-1980's)

Circleport Office Park—Erlanger, Kentucky (Mid-1980s)

Orlando Central Park I & II—Orlando, FL (Late 1980's)

Platinum Tower
Atlanta, GA 1987

Towers of Rivercenter—1988 to 2001

Cincinnati Bell Training Facility—Erlanger, KY 1990

One Renaissance Center & Government Service Center Garage Hamilton, OH 1997

Marriott Rivercenter Covington, KY—1999

Madison Place/Domaine De La Rive—Covington, KY 2001

Denver Art Museum Residences—2006

Humana Headquarters/Baldwin Building—2007
Cincinnati, Ohio

Baldwin Complex—2008

The Ascent—2008

Aloft Hotel—Phoenix 2009

Alpine Mountain Ranch

Main Entrance Gate—2010

The Hermitage—2010

Lodge—2010

Model Home—2015

Model Home—2017

Guest Cabins—2022

The building is truly artful, both externally and internally. It has won many awards. Condé Nast has named it one of the 20 best hotels in the world, and Tripadvisor has repeatedly named it the number one hotel in all of Colorado.

In some ways, we went overboard, yet we still managed to deliver the property on a reasonable cost basis. But every detail, every element has been carefully addressed with a sense of uniqueness. We hired Leo Villareal, the lighting engineer who has created attractions on the Bay Bridge in San Francisco and at the Smithsonian and National Gallery of Art in Washington, D.C., to install a cloud of moving lights under the arrival canopy. It is one-of-a-kind, and people are completely awestruck as they arrive and open their car doors.

The property opened for business in 2016, but as business was ramping up, the pandemic hit. Occupancy in downtown hotels dropped from 78 percent to 10 percent. We toughed it out with the help of our lenders and additional contributions of capital, and we are now in the second year of rebuilding the business revenues. The ART is a beautiful property and is now recovering but, as with all hotels, struggling with increased costs of both food and people.

Banking Revisited: American Founders Bank

Given my earlier experiences investing in the Southern Ohio Bank, I should have learned, but it would seem I cannot resist the banking business. Ten years earlier, when I was working on getting a convention center for Northern Kentucky at Rivercenter, I came to know a man named Brereton Jones, who was running for governor of Kentucky. Brereton was not only the governor of Kentucky but also a prominent thoroughbred horse breeder in central Kentucky. I supported him in his political race and, once in office, he did indeed give our community the Northern Kentucky Convention Center, which accelerated the development of Covington along the river. He and I worked closely on multiple projects while he was in office, and we maintained a relationship after he left office in 1995. Once Brereton was out of office, I invested in a few of his horse syndications.

In 2002 Brereton and another entrepreneur were forming a new bank corporation, American Founders Bank, and raised $6 million in capital. I invested $250,000 for a 4 percent interest. I did not take a seat on the board. The first decade of the millennium was very robust for banking, and this bank grew from its initial $6 million in assets to nearly $330 million in a six- to seven-year period. We at Corporex were busy as well and I paid limited attention. As the bank rapidly grew during those boom years, it was necessary to add equity investments to stay within regulatory requirements, and the management issued more stock each time rebalancing occurred. I made additional pro rata equity investments each time, as they were booking profit—and went on about our business.

Then the management and board took a leap. American Founders Bank acquired another bank, doubling its size overnight. In 2007, it borrowed $16 million from US Bank and issued another $25 million of what is known as "Trust Preferred" stock, essentially disguised debt, to acquire First Security Bank of Lexington, Kentucky.

One year later, Brereton called for help. He needed to replace the CEO quickly, and confidentially, so I introduced him to a man at PNC Bank with whom I had recent discussions about buying a different small bank. John Taylor took the job. The entire banking industry in America was by this time in turmoil following the 2008 financial meltdown, and the management of American Founders had choked on integrating the two enterprises into one. Long story short, as I had a lot of confidence in John, once he was in place, I made even larger investments alongside Brereton and Tracy Farmer, the chairman and other of the founders in order to capitalize the company further and to, in essence, save the bank.

In the end, I had to write off the entire stock investments, taking a big loss. The only money I hoped to retrieve was a $1 million loan I had made, as did Brereton, in addition to the shares of stock from investing. The bank continued to suffer badly as the Great Recession deepened. The burden of the debt to acquire First Security plus the bad loans coming forth were too much. After writing off my investment a number of years later, I came to realize that the bank was, in essence, being slowly liquidated and our $1 million loans also were in jeopardy. That prompted me to take action.

US Bank's loan was paid down to $13.5 million and was fully secured by the stock of the bank itself. The other lenders, meaning those owning "Trust Preferred" shares, were out of luck; their trust-preferred shares were worthless. US Bank felt the value of its loan was also nearly worthless. I had a longtime relationship with US Bank, so I called and offered them $1 million to buy their $13.5 million position. My thinking was that if I could get into their shoes, I could then have more control over what happens to the bank; the bank officers would have to come to me for approval on every major event. I still was not on the board, nor did I want to be.

We filed for a 363 restructuring process (so named for Section 363 of the U.S. Bankruptcy Code), which is used for banks in straits like this. A 363 Sale filing is essentially the same as filing for Chapter 11 bankruptcy except it does not sound so bad in the eyes of the public and the name of the bank does not get tarnished as in bankruptcy. In brief, once we had come out of bankruptcy, having sold two-thirds of the remaining loan assets on the books to a West Virginia bank together with the Lexington headquarters building, I relocated this very small bank with $120 million in total assets to Louisville, a market three times larger than Lexington but with essentially the same competitors. I was somewhat excited to come full circle to do business in Louisville again—it was sentimental.

But growing a small bank is difficult, and after two years of limited success, I decided to sell, if possible. We did end up selling it in 2018 to a large credit union in Evansville, Indiana, that wanted an operation and headquarters building in Louisville. We successfully negotiated a price of $18.5 million. So I got my entire original investment back, the additional money to buy the loan, and approximately $7 million on top of it.

In addition, we sold only the financial assets and the real estate but kept the American Founders Bank corporate entity, with its big tax loss credits valued at approximately $26 million. That amount I could then carry forward against future income that we could generate. Those losses are worth a net value of

$7 million to $8 million in cash tax obligations we could offset. So, subsequently, we used the residual capital to acquire our affiliate hotel management company, which could potentially absorb those tax credits over the following seven years.

Commonwealth Hotels, Inc., our hotel management enterprise, is now owned by the corporation that was once a bank. Buying that note from US Bank was creative and extremely risky, but turned out to be a good idea with a really great outcome. Only a determined entrepreneur would do such a thing, but I did not want to lose the other money I had loaned to the bank.

Against All Odds—Four Major Recessions of Our Time

When one who has lived the ups and downs looks over the past, what stands out are the painful moments that had to be overcome—mainly caused by recessions—but also the changes that came forth in response to those periods in time. Corporex experienced an unusual number of relatively severe downturns in building the business over the years. I counted that of the first 50 years we were in business, 19 years, or nearly 40 percent of the time, were during serious recessionary periods, and then a pandemic, an event difficult to label. I think for any evolving business of any type to have to navigate through that many years of economic downturns of such severity is rare. Moreover, commercial developers experience deeper and higher impacts than most businesses—higher peaks, deeper crevices, it seems, likely due to the nature of the business itself.

On at least two occasions, we essentially tore down the company and rebuilt it again. I regret immensely that we had two painful layoffs in our 57 years. They were unavoidable if the company was to survive those downturns. Otherwise, we have been proud to say that we have been able to preserve jobs during most of the economic cycles.

One was the 1973–1975 contraction, sometimes referred to as a correction, caused by the oil embargo. It was sharp—surprisingly so. The downturn was like walking off a cliff. Corporations literally terminated building contracts midstream, with construction underway. If a committed contract had not yet been finalized, it would not be.

We had major contracts cancelled. And the subcontractors refused to honor their commitments for roofing and asphalt paving even though they were under written contract, because those trades were connected to oil for their products and the increased costs of the material rendered their contract with us a losing proposition. We had no choice but to pay another contractor a larger amount and incur a loss ourselves. We entered that recession with 181 field people, 38 office staff members, and an approximate $5 million backlog of construction. To survive, we laid off all but two of the field people and all but 11 of the office folks. I took no salary or draw for at least two years.

The 1980–1982 recession was severe in a reverse way; I always referred to it as the upside-down recession. Commercial property development relies heavily on mortgage leverage, or borrowing money for 75–85 percent of the cost to build the property. If interest rates cost 20 percent, the carry costs during construction and lease-up will double one's initial cost in only four to five years. As I indicated, there was no shortage of money, but we grew in this period for other reasons and with a long-term perspective. Notwithstanding, it was a treacherous environment.

But 1990–1995, "the credit crunch debacle," was the worst period ever we had to navigate, because we were much larger by then and had 10 times the debt load to carry. In order to survive, we were forced to unwind, reverse the employment process once again by shrinking from 267 salaried people to 77, and close two offices, in just a 12-month period. It was devastating for us as management and especially for me as CEO who had interviewed most of those people, offered them an opportunity. But if we had not acted in a dramatic way, there would be no Corporex today.

An Appointment with the Pope, Cancelled?

February 1993, the middle of the commercial real estate credit crunch meltdown, was Sue's and my 25th wedding anniversary. Wanting to help us mark the occasion, Corporex's Bill Blackham (with the help of Cardinal Law from Boston and our local Bishop Hughes) arranged for a special invitation from the Vatican to attend Pope John Paul II's private morning mass in the Pope's residence.

It was a sacred opportunity, and Sue and I felt blessed to be asked. However, something arose almost daily that year that threatened the company's existence. As our trip date loomed, something came up, so I cancelled on the Pope. Everyone around me was shocked. My wife was not very happy, nor was I, but this surprising decision gives some insight into this period in our history and the stress and urgency that we lived with.

Well, the appointment got rescheduled months later, and Sue and I did, in fact, have a wonderful experience attending his morning mass and meeting Pope John Paul II afterward. continuing formation, and in particular how I relate to the Church since.

People have often asked me what impact this event had on me. I came away with one significant takeaway: When the Catholic Church speaks out on moral issues or religious policies, it is not a simple matter. When the Pope speaks, the message will be received differently by the 165 countries and cultures in the world. So it is not an easy task to lead the world on such important and earth-moving matters. I came to realize why the Church is slow to change. As a result, I have become more patient with the Catholic Church. I've tried to be more understanding about why it cannot move quickly or become more current in teaching, as the congregation in America has pushed for. That is my biggest takeaway, while it was truly a special spiritual experience for both of us.

Although our audience with the Pope had to be rescheduled due to the economic turmoil at home, following each of these severe economic corrections, we redirected and remade the company, heading into somewhat different directions each time as a result of the experience and the changes to the daily practices of society and business. We had to change because in the after winds of every recession, there is some order of structural remodeling to the overall economy. And, indeed, that is the case with the most recent and extended correction.

The fourth big recession of our career, which we have mentioned previously, came along in 2008 was unusually long, earning it the name Great Recession. I did not expect such a long recovery, and our partner Andy Daly and I even held a forum in Steamboat Springs in 2010 to express our bullishness on the recovery based on historical charts. But no, this one caused a slog effect.

Fortunately, as in 1989 when we sold a portfolio of properties to Equitable Life in advance of the previous credit crunch period, we took action in a similar way in late 2007 when we sold Eagle Hospitality Property Trust, the publicly traded hotel company, to Apollo Real Estate. The timing of this sale appears in retrospect as genius but in reality, it was just the outcome of doing the right thing for the right reasons, and it filled our coffers again with the ability to carry through another severe downturn.

When I look back summarily over the entire history of the company, what is prominent to the emotions are these trying, stress-filled times; thus, the title *Into the Wind*.

It was more than just sheer determination that allowed us to prevail against such winds. We did not just try to get through those times, even though insuring that we did was foremost on our minds. We also attacked in a number of ways when others were retreating. But we always believed that in every problem there was an opportunity, and a number of strategies emerged that we came to rely on. For example, "all hands on deck" was an often-employed rallying call that we repeated to emphasize urgency. Then there was the Parnelli Jones strategy. Not everyone knows Parnelli Jones, the famous Indy-car driver, but he was relevant because of how he raced through the streets. While most people instinctively put their foot on the brake when facing a problem to constrain spending during recessions, which we did, we also kept the other foot on the accelerator to continue moving forward. To apply this practice has always been our way in recession periods. And quite often opportunities are created out of problematic, even crisis, situations. It is important to be alert during the downturns; to spot opportunities requires an intentional effort to that end. The opportunity we found in Denver during the depths of the 2008–09 debacle, Fitzsimons Village is a perfect example of such discipline.

We did not want to lose valuable years to any downturn, so, instead, we found a way to advance while remaining ready to pump the brakes. Each time we came out the other end, we progressed, usually in multiple directions and dimensions, not just revenue growth. For example, the personnel we recruited, the policies we implemented from our lessons, larger projects completed and bigger goals set. We were determined to make up for lost opportunities in those difficult periods where we had to batten down the hatches. We always wanted to improve ourselves as a consequence of those lessons, and I think we did.

An even bigger factor in our survival, moreover in our success over time, may have been our long-term perspective and our ability to see beyond the challenging periods we were immersed in. Having a very long-term perspective has allowed us to weather the storms. Decisions and investments based on long-term objectives have always been the dominant criteria for the way we have managed the business, reinforced by various lessons I learned over the years, including a fantastic one from Europe.

Once, while I was in Germany in 1978, a bank official took me to a room where his investment team traded securities. This was during the hyperinflation years. The entire walls of the room were painted with a graph, a chart that plotted the American market history against the European economies. European economies have existed for nearly 3,000 years, while the United States at the time had just passed 200. In other words, the Europeans could read us like a book. They did not get so unnerved by our recessions, having seen their own over many more centuries. Using their knowledge, they could invest in timely ways.

Another Eye-Opener

Among other experiences of that trip, a lesson was brought home to me in Munich when I decided to knock on the door of a commercial office developer whose headquarters was near my hotel. He had developed many commercial buildings in this sector, and while I did not get to the top guy, the second-in-command agreed to see me. We compared notes about an office building that I was building versus one he had just completed. He could quickly convert measurements of meters versus feet and inches, and marks, their currency, versus dollars. I told him my land was $100,000 per acre. He computed and converted his land costs and said his land was the equivalent of $2.5 million per acre—25 times more. His costs per square foot to construct the tower were $265 (in 1978) compared to mine at $70. His rents were $15 per square foot compared to mine at $11 at the time. I said something like, "This is incredible, how can you invest in such a property for so little return?" He answered, "We do not! We build for the insurance companies. They are happy if the property achieves break-even revenue in 15 or 20 years. Then if we make some money over time by developing for them, we might build a small building for our own account." Talk about long-term perspective, but then I think that is what is happening in the U.S. in current times. There are huge takeaways in this simple example, especially when one examines the disparity of his land values at 25 times versus the building construction cost difference to ours at only four times. Land is a limited commodity and can be precious.

As economies grow, and they must by design, profit margins are compressed and one's investment horizons must change. We have to think in terms of longer periods of returns, holding assets for many years. Economic compression is what squeezes out smaller companies and prevents entrepreneurial individuals like me from going into business. It takes much more operating capital today to sustain over the longer investment horizons.

Following the pandemic of 2020–2022, we experienced rising inflation similar to the mid-1970s, and investment rates that would suggest America has reached a different scale of thinking, similar to what I had observed with the German developer. At the time I met the gentleman, interest rates were upwards of 8 percent, yet their long-term investment philosophy surrounding real estate was based on 1–2 percent initial investment yields. We have seen similar numbers recently, now 45 years later.

I bite my tongue whenever I say, "I could not do what we did at Corporex again, not in these years compared to when I began in the 1960s, at least not in the real estate development and investment field." In Europe, starting a business at a young age like I did is much more difficult due to the bureaucracy within their economies. A start-up would require 10 times the financial resources I had to get revenues activated.

I Am Not Building an Estate— I Am Building a Company

Likely the strongest factor in our being able to operate the business through thick and thin was built into our foundational business philosophy.

I am reminded of sitting in meetings of the National Association of Industrial Parks with other developers from around the country in the late 1970s. We were being schooled about our personal wealth projections by the experts. Inflation was soaring in the 1970s, and real estate valuations were projected to rise to lofty levels. The others around the table were concerned about their estates and the taxes they would incur. The discussion among the various entrepreneurs at the event was intense and focused. However, I didn't have the same reaction at all, and others in the group took notice. Finally, one person at the table asked why I was not concerned. My response was, "I am not building an estate. I am building a company. If I am successful at building a good company, I will eventually have a big estate tax problem—and I will deal with it then."

This focus on building a business is why we held Corporex's investment properties in a traditional corporation, while others owned their real estate in their own name or in partnerships outside the corporation. That, too, made all the difference in those difficult days. We were able to offset tax losses with gains by consolidating our assets in a single corporate framework, filing consolidated tax returns. That could not be accomplished in separated entities with multiple owners. The Trammell Crow partners, for example, were not able to offset and would often incur income tax obligations from mortgage forgiveness when they were foreclosed upon by lenders, while at the same time there would be no cash available to pay these taxes. It forced some into bankruptcy filings, and their properties to be sold for big losses at auction.

Although we were structured as a private corporation, we operated with the discipline of a publicly traded enterprise and have published audited financial statements consistently since 1975. We publish them in an annual report that rivals those of public companies, in four-color, printed and bound. This investment in the annual reporting process created a sense of responsibility and comfort to our many bankers and demonstrated our prowess as business executives, not just as real estate entrepreneurs.

Yes, we did prevail and succeed against the odds of four major and deep recessions and one pandemic in our time, always with an eye toward the future.

All Roads Lead to Ovation!

It is becoming known as an "Urban Resort," a term which speaks to the full embodiment of the lifestyle as well as the positioning of this activity center along the confluence of not one but two rivers. Ovation! is more than initially meets the eye. It is a true living, working, entertainment development unlike anything seen in any middle-American metro. Understanding the full value, the feel, the experience of living or working in Ovation! on the part of the wider population will simply take years, no matter how we may undertake to accelerate the process. Once completed, Ovation! will give rise to a changed perception of the entire urban sector of the entire population center we call Greater Cincinnati, including the Northern Kentucky areas.

Ovation! is the biggest endeavor Corporex has ever tackled, and clearly a leading-edge action. In the end, more than $1 billion will have been invested in buildings and structures alone to create a large-scale, multifaceted community project. The master plan's footprint covers the equivalent of 17 urban acres, which Corporex currently owns, with another five peripheral acres within Corporex's exclusive development agreement. A downtown city block in most cities is approximately 400 feet by 400 feet, which means that Ovation! is the equivalent of 4.6 city blocks, built atop two-level parking structures and a unique full roadway system on the platform above. That is a big undertaking for a community of our nature and size. It could not be accomplished without an extraordinary and overarching commitment, as well as special financial incentives to overcome marginal economic returns that justify and support funding.

Novel tax legislation was created in Kentucky during the governorship of Ernie Fletcher. I am proud to say we had a strong hand in Governor Fletcher's successful election because he beat out the man who as Kentucky's attorney general had initiated the sham grand jury process surrounding the so-called "Kenton County Bidding Scandal" in the late '90s. But I am also proud of having helped craft the most unique tax increment financing (TIF) in the United States. TIFs allow a developer to use a portion of the new "incremental" tax revenues generated by the project, and sometimes its surrounds, to retire debts and capital employed to make the project happen. Without Kentucky's signature legislation, multiple projects in the Commonwealth of Kentucky simply could not have happened. Ovation! is one of 24 TIF-induced projects around the state underway currently.

There is a special provision within this legislation called a "Signature TIF" that applies only to super-sized development projects like Ovation! The project has to have spent $200 million capital-invested to trigger collection of the taxes. In our case, the legislation has incentivized a project that is five times the minimum threshold. I remember consulting for the then-president of the Kentucky Senate very late on a Saturday night to craft the creative language of the law.

That was more than 15 years ago. I also recall that after the bill was passed, the following week he announced: "We have passed a piece of legislation that will cause projects that will be seen from outer-space." I know for sure that I will not ever get to see Ovation! from that perspective, but I hope he is right. Indeed, to my knowledge, there is no comparable statewide tax incentive legislation in the entire United States. So long as it remains on the books, Kentucky's progress will be accelerated.

We purchased the site in 2006 for twice the amount any other bidder was willing to pay. Of course, no other bidder had the scale of vision that was in my mind. So the price we paid represented just over 1 percent of the entire investment we envisioned. But our acquisition closed just in time for another recession to hit, which would shut down new real estate development for, at a minimum, eight years. We hired several architectural firms to carry out our vision on paper in a design competition approach. We liked one of the designs by a firm out of Cleveland. As is customary, this design would have to be modified until we arrived at a plan we felt comfortable with. What we are building today, in 2022, looks nothing like that original plan.

The recession that started in 2008 was severe and deep. There was a sense of panic in the financial markets. The Obama administration put forth legislation to feed money into the economy in what became known as funding for "shovel-ready projects." The State of Kentucky reached out to the City of Newport to identify opportunities to put this money to work quickly. The city, in turn, reached out to us, and we sprang into action by working with the Kentucky Department of Transportation to design a new boulevard into and through our development site. This roadway would connect arterial traffic patterns from east to west and would tie into Route 9, already under construction, which would extend to the southern reaches of the county. Today this artery is complete, and the amount of traffic it carries is significant already. But shovel-ready apparently meant different time horizons to different people, as the Commonwealth of Kentucky did nothing more than acquired the right of way under eminent domain, and did not act on building the roadway for more than eight years. Our project was frozen as a result. We had completely revised our development plan to work around the new roadway, and without assurance it would actually be constructed, neither we nor any financial partner could move forward. Our hands were tied not only by the recession but also by this bureaucratic delay. It was a period where our governor at the time favored other parts of the state with whatever funds were available. Finally, it happened, and our development got underway in 2018.

Phase one of the project is near completion as this is written in 2023. It involves an elevated plaza, a state-of-the-art music venue for up to 6,000 people on the exterior side—on a sloped grass amphitheater built atop the garage—plus 2,800 people both standing and sitting on the interior. As many as 400,000 adults are expected to visit the Ovation! entertainment pavilion each year, which activity will go a long way toward supporting the retail and entertainment spread throughout the master plan. The first of at least two office towers and the first of three hotels are well underway, as phase two is currently rising out of the ground.

Phase two of three represents an investment of nearly $100 million in itself to build an 1,800-car structure with a drivable platform on top. It will be an incredibly complex project involving more than 1,000 residential units, both apartments and single owner, two more office buildings, special hotels, and a private club. A resort-style swimming pool will actually be built on the elevated plaza. Two exciting public places will cause the project to come alive: the Boardwalk and Illumination Square. Corporex is building an authentic boardwalk along the levy, which runs along the river on the front of the project. Restaurants, bars, and other entertainment features will line the boardwalk. Community gatherings will occur in another exciting space, an interior courtyard called Illumination Square. The views of the Cincinnati skyline over top of the river are awesome, especially when the city is lit at night. The Bengals' Paul Brown Stadium and the Cincinnati Reds' Great American Ball Park appear front and center.

There is a central theme to our thoughts as we design the components of this development of living. We named it CASA (as in the Spanish word for home):In our case C stands for color, A for art, S for sound, and A for architecture. Weaving all of these elements together in the correct matrix is our stated endeavor, together with safety and other more customary expectations one would normally incorporate.

When we broke ground on the amazing Ascent project in 2005, I said loosely, "Considering the Ascent's dynamic architectural presentation, this one will be our last hurrah!" And, again, I was wrong. It turns out the Ascent is only a small fraction of the scope of Ovation!

In more ways than one building can do, Ovation! will be the biggest hurrah of this man's career, and a proud accomplishment for the Corporex teams of people who will carry out the full vision. We are well aware that in our geographic locale, it may take as long as 15–20 years to completely build out, but Ovation! will forever change the skyline. It has been suggested that the project may be the one last piece of the puzzle, so to speak, that will overcome the schism of cultural difference between the Ohio and Kentucky sides of the big river. With the help of Ovation! we may finally "bridge the bridges."

Cincinnati will want to claim Ovation! as part of its urban core, but Ovation! and Rivercenter too, are in Kentucky, so Cincinnatians will have to claim Kentucky and its people too. The two will not become one but, in spirit, we will become more in oneness. We, together, will be much more accepting and willing to act collectively. Physical developments can have that type of effect long term, but it is but one step toward a unified community at a regional level.

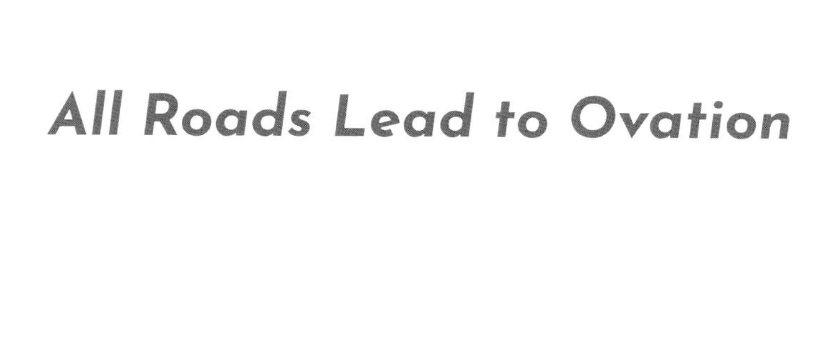
All Roads Lead to Ovation

STEAK HOUSE

RESTAURANT.

Part III

Builder of People

"It is not large revenues or number of employees that distinguish Corporex, those were never our measures. It is its deep purpose—from the outset."

—WILLIAM P. BUTLER

Chapter 14

Valuable Trade-offs

There is nothing more rewarding for a guy like me than to look upon the success of people who worked with him over the years, who have grown in confidence and skill, in lifestyle and purpose as a consequence of their experience and tenure with our company. Promotions for advancement are only one measure of success. Personal growth, expanded mindset, spiritual and inner-strength discovery—these attributes manifest what truly counts in my view of a person's success. They also give witness to the company's overarching benefit to its people.

Corporex could have been a much larger company, but being large was never the ultimate goal. Neither was being wealthy. By opting not to build an empire and to focus on good work rather than outsized profits, we were able to provide greater opportunities for more people. If wealth and size had been our primary missions or purpose, we would have done things much differently at every step.

Wealth scared me, always did. I was forever cognizant of that biblical passage about the rich man being unable to get through "the eye of the needle." That stuck with me, I think, embedded. But so is the promise I made on October 11, 1964, at 3:30 in the afternoon, while alone in a chapel with one flickering candle. The challenge for me from that date forward was to weave into the corporate fabric the concept of service and purpose, and a mission that fulfilled that fateful "I do"; the commitment I earnestly made on that Cursillo retreat weekend.

This meant Corporex had to be outreaching, charitable, and other-focused as a company. We had to be highly ethical, moral, service-oriented, and generous, especially to those whom we call the "less hopeful." So too, we had to be dedicated to the people who relied on us for their livelihood. So I set out to become a weaver of sorts, to marry capitalism and Christian outreach in an integrated manner. I knew this would be a large challenge, but for me it was essential: a promise, a commitment. I did not know how that might play out, so it was in some way a matter of blind faith.

Giving money is one thing. Giving time is yet another, maybe more expensive, commodity, because it sidetracks one's attention from corporate goals. Some corporations, in particular publicly traded entities, discourage their people from getting involved deeply in civic and community actions, sitting on boards. Corporex does not. Of course, all acts of this nature must be prudently managed, but in general we support any of our employees' efforts to serve those in need. For example, throughout each year, the employee group conducts philanthropic drives to provide assistance to the less advantaged, usually during Thanksgiving and the Christmas season. But recently, the group decided to form its own donor-advised fund at our Horizon Community Funds public charity, where payroll deductions can occur, and where the employees themselves determine how contributions should be distributed year-round. This new fund provides Corporex team members with a more fulfilling role. The company will provide matching grants as a way to partner with team members and increase their impact.

In addition to the blind faith of my born-again experience, the core values taught by my parents, the priests, and the nuns combined with my inherent idealism to shape the Corporex culture. Those traits are still alive and in fact play a big role in how we manage the company. Thanks to my early life preparation, at Corporex we have always had stretch goals, have always sought high-touch in all things: quality and progressive design, dress code, depth of service to our customers. Some have criticized us for being perfectionists, being overly demanding and unreasonable—but it was all in search of excellence.

The Corporex Culture

I am not proud to say that 56 years in business passed without stopping to take stock in what we call the culture of Corporex. However, I am proud of that culture as we have come to understand it. I feel confident we lived and leaned upon our culture, but we never attempted to discover it, or to highlight it, or to document it. Only recently, as I have tried to step aside into what we sometimes refer to as my "rewirement," have we zeroed in on identifying the Corporex culture. I wish I had done so many years earlier, as we would be an even stronger organization with even more success today. We would have recruited people specifically with our culture in mind, more effectively seeking those who closely shared our values. We have discovered that the people who stay with us long term—there have been quite a few—already prioritized those unique elements of our corporate culture. But my disappointment with not addressing culture was about then; now is now.

We recently assembled a professionally produced and bound book, *Make No Little Plans*, which embodies the nine foundational components of our unique corporate culture. Two of its themes are "discovering our inner strengths" and how a corporation can be "more than a financial enterprise." My one last big goal is for Corporex to go forward another 50-plus years. Defining and owning our unique culture will be essential to those who carry the company into the future.

I find corporate culture is often confused and misunderstood. Different individuals describe and define it differently, depending on their own makeup and perspective. The too-often-heard response to the question is that culture is all about work environment, perks and benefits, and the likes and dislikes of people, personalities. Those are significant but to me somewhat shallow and do not contain the energy that drives dreamers and doers.

Studies of Corporex and of the most successful companies reveal there is much more to culture, including management disciplines, work ethic, mission and purpose, defined service commitment, and other material contributors.

When we stopped to address the topic, we discovered those traits that have made all the difference in who we are. We learned what in our culture distinguishes us and that, as a company, we want to be much more than merely a financial enterprise.

We identified the overarching characteristics of Corporex culture to be, first and foremost, centered on one word: **quality**. Then eight more foundational principles in no particular order:

- Quality in all things
- Strong work ethic
- Commitment to growth
- Disciplined, but with flexibility
- Entrepreneurial urgency
- A supportive environment (internally)
- Creative and innovative
- Long-term perspective
- Community outreach

These are in addition to employee-focused programs and recognitions that, in my view, add personality to the underlying culture. I did not mention security, another employee benefit. But we take a different approach to security—we call it growth! We have always believed that personal security of an individual comes from within the person themselves and that no programs in a highly productive enterprise can provide security in its truest terms or application. But we do believe that continuous growth, challenge, and advancement from one's own success in meeting those challenges is what gives rise to enhanced self-esteem, self-confidence, fulfillment of the individual, and, most important, dignity. Those who attain these attributes are secure in themselves as a result. And success in these cultural attributes breeds personal happiness. Accordingly, we have always felt it our responsibility to provide expansionary challenge, continuing growth opportunities, as a serious element of our corporate culture.

I cannot think of a stronger benefit a company can deliver for its employees than these ingredients. That is, when the business supports its people in such a way that they grow from their successes, that they are challenged and meet those challenges, and they become confident, fulfilled, and inherently secure in themselves, therein lies dignity, one of my favorite terms. And amidst their progress, of course, financial recognition. Money in savings is essential, but it is more valuable when it is earned. Corporex is committed to growth in great measure, expressly with an eye to this benefit to our people.

Quality, the very first trait, drives everything within our business: the buildings we design and build, our business park developments, the relationships of trust we develop, our reach for excellence in all things, including selecting our customers, partners, relationships at all levels, the people we recruit. Quality is at the center of our pride.

We refer often to entrepreneurial urgency. We are truly an entrepreneurial company. Ours is a higher-than-average-risk business by nature and thus requires high energy. One cannot succeed—not well, not in the development business—without a sense of urgency. Too often the boss's sense of urgency in setting performance dates is interpreted negatively as demanding, but without urgency, the grass grows, deals are lost, and windows in the economy are missed at great expense. Our development projects often begin in one economic cycle and come to market in a changed economic environment. Not only do we have to be somewhat visionary in forecasting, we need to be industrious to deliver before the downturns.

We are known for being supportive and collaborative. Without reservation, one trait that makes Corporex different is that there is no infighting or jockeying for position among our people—no back-biting. It is not because we preach on this topic, it just happens in the environment we have created. Folks who tend to engage in gossip and rumor-mongering tend to be uncomfortable and leave the company well before they are asked to do so. We are also known for being supportive, occasionally to a fault, giving people plenty of room to succeed, to learn, to grow, and to change their habits if necessary—to perform, so long as they are trying in earnest. We know this is expensive, but it is our way. It is an element of our commitment to the people of Corporex.

Ours is a strong work ethic. Hard work is one of the pillars of Corporex and its culture. We openly advise that if you do not place yourself in the category of being an above average achiever and above average worker, then do not seek a position with our company. Corporex has always been a place for those who seek out growth, those who have purpose in their life, those who want to be known for their contribution.

In the early days of the company, I often referred to myself as a task master, believing I was, as they say, very demanding in my expectations. Of course, that demanding nature reflected my self-expectations, which unquestionably carried over to those around me. My example set the tone, and many times the dates I set for task completion seemed unreasonable to others. But there was no choice. We began without money and were running for years against a daily threat of cash shortages; we had to outrun economics, and fortunately that is just what we did. But, of course, this made productivity paramount—except for the principle of quality, which was never infringed upon no matter how hard the times. That has led to stretch goals and elements of urgency as a steady component of our corporate diet; those attributes have served us well over many years of volatile economic forces.

Our culture, while not defined up front, was the medicine that carried us through to the other side each time.

We cherish that we are an entrepreneurial company, a risk-taking company, an opportunistic enterprise, too. It is fun to seek out opportunity, which is often discovered by seeking an unfilled service, or created by developing an improved way to deliver a service or product. It is very American, indeed, to be an entrepreneurial risk taker. It is challenging and, if done prudently, is rewarding in more than a financial sense.

Often developers are viewed as gamblers. Some who call themselves developers are indeed gamblers; but not Corporex, not Bill Butler. I have emphatically asserted on multiple occasions that I am a big risk-taker. In fact, to make a point, I make the statement, "I am a huge risk-taker. I love risk—but I am not a gambler." Not at all. There is a difference.

A well-respected CPA from Arthur Andersen once told me years ago, "Bill, the difference between Corporex and every other developer I serve is the risk-reward spread in your projects." It struck home. We have always protected the downside first and foremost, and strived on the other hand to enhance the upside potential with an equal commitment. This created a measure of insurance against the risk. Gamblers do not protect the downside. In fact, they are often incapable of seeing the downside. For this reason, those who are truly gamblers do not move with urgency, and predictably fail. We are big risk takers, but we are not gamblers.

Plant Your Head Up High in the Clouds, Keep Your Feet Firmly on the Ground

A tenet of Corporex has always been to help people achieve more than they may have thought they could. Architectural design is an area of the business where we have always excelled. Young architects on multiple occasions joined the company and were given a deadline to completely develop the design of a building within, say, one week or 10 days so that we could prepare our estimates and quotations for the prospective buyer within two weeks. Just to prepare the cost estimate for a bid in two weeks is considered a feat, but we did it consistently. The architect would discover that his or her best creativity rises against a strong deadline, completes the assignment, and then comes to realize that what was asked could, in fact, be accomplished—and, as a result, the individual felt a new sense of confidence. We also work closely with third-party architectural firms and, to a great degree, we find our challenges to them—setting deadlines, painting idealistic purpose—has proven to bring forth some extraordinary designs, as evidenced by our numerous awards.

Over the years we have received letters from former employees—we call them alumni—who came to realize what Corporex was all about, how they had advanced due to our culture, and from the challenges that were afforded them while employed here, even commending our disciplined ways, which they missed in other firms. But they had to leave Corporex to realize these attributes and how much they had grown. It is always nice when someone shares such thoughts. In most cases, they are not asking to return and, in fact, find themselves prepared to do their current jobs with advantages relative to their peers. But some have returned over time, and we have always welcomed them back when we had the right opportunity.

There is no doubt that culture has been key to our success. To excel in the future, we came to realize that we needed to move it to the forefront to emphasize what makes us different. We like our cultural distinctions, and we believe they must be verbalized often, and also serve as a guide internally for hiring and for all that we conduct as executives and managers day to day. In my view, honoring these elements could take Corporex from a being good company to a being great company.

One of my personal missions has been developing, challenging, educating, and encouraging people to be the best they can be. My most fulfilling thoughts, as I look back, are those that reflect on the successes of people who stretched and succeeded here at Corporex. The culture of Corporex is such that a person must be inclined to grow, must be going somewhere with their life in order to thrive here. Now that I have reached a hefty age, I enjoy regularly scheduled mentoring sessions with the up-and-coming leaders within the company—and I find the up and comers are eager to meet and open to discussion. This is rewarding to me. This is fun.

It is also important to emphasize that the successes we have experienced as a company are due to not just a few but to the many hard-working people who have contributed over and above what was asked of them, with loyalty over many years. We have been blessed with truly great people in our family of companies, and I am very grateful to have known and worked with them side by side through the years.

There is no doubt that their contributions, their collective personas, make up our corporate DNA. Who we are, who Corporex is in the future, will continue to be the product of the personalities, desires, and natural skills of those who find their pathways at Corporex well into the future.

Community outreach is one of the most important components of Corporex's culture. It is part of the foundation on which the company was established. And in many ways, it is one of the most rewarding elements of our hard work and our personality as a company. The focus on people extends beyond those who rely on Corporex for compensation and livelihood to those less hopeful in our communities. In this regard, we have defined our communities to be wherever we find ourselves and from which we gain. To those places we are committed to provide outreach. Several of the most significant people-focused organizations that we have fostered and aligned with are in our hometown.

Chapter 15

Fruits of the Enterprise

Many years ago, Sue and I incorporated a tax-exempt, private charitable foundation. Various Corporex companies contribute to this foundation annually as part of their operating budgets, and in the economic uptimes, we fund more than usual.

The Butler Foundation

The Butler Foundation has become a significant entity, partnering with other similar foundations to yield bigger outcomes for the community. The early thinking behind its establishment was that by building up a corpus of giving during the good times, we would have a reservoir of funds to be able to draw on during the more difficult times when the struggling members of society in our community needed it the most. Too often people give only when they have a good year; we decided to front-load our charity so we could also give during the down cycles.

The foundation was originally meant to spotlight my parents, especially since Dad had been so generous in his life. My brother Marty and I acknowledge when we reminisce that Dad was our model for giving. Marty is chairman of the foundation, and his children, ours, and several nephews and nieces, are on the board. Originally chartered the Robert M. and Martha F. Butler Memorial Foundation, the name was cumbersome and long, so eventually we changed it simply to the Butler Foundation. The foundation is well known throughout Northern Kentucky and Cincinnati for its very brief mission statement: "To get the money to the people who need it the most, through the most direct way possible."

The foundation is primarily focused on hardship grants. Educational scholarships for youth are a big focus, we support multiple social service programs, and we also concentrate on a variety of projects designed to move the community forward. I know we have changed many lives, but when we have the opportunity to hear firsthand from those the foundation has served, it reignites this commitment to bettering the residents of our community.

I had one such experience approximately eight to ten years ago when a handsome young man approached me while Sue and I were having dinner at an outdoor café. He walked over to our table and asked, "Are you Mr. Butler ?" "Yes," I told him, and we continued getting acquainted. I asked him what he did for work. "I am a brand manager for Procter & Gamble. Actually, I am responsible for two brands," he told us. I said, "Wow, you seem young to be a brand manager from what I know about P&G." "Well, I put in my time in Europe, Asia, and South America learning the people," he told us.

Then he went on, "You probably don't remember this, but you paid my way through college." You can imagine how I felt, and still feel, when telling this story. Frankly, the feeling is so full it is difficult to describe. It is difficult to repeat this conversation without tearing up. This executive was the epitome of what we had hoped the Butler Foundation would do for members of our community—provide a way to better their lives by giving opportunities to those who would otherwise not be able to avail themselves of such doors to their future.

This executive graduated from Northern Kentucky University, where we maintain a large scholarship fund for those who would be unable to get a degree without some help. The Foundation promises to support our Butler Scholars provided they continue to achieve a threshold grade point average, and we will do it every year beginning in high school should we get started with them at an earlier age. Apparently, we did it for this man many years prior.

As its resources have grown, the Foundation has expanded from education to include other high-impact programs, such as the Life Learning Center and the Samaritan Car Care Clinic.

There are too many not-for-profit agencies we have supported over the years to recite. Before establishing the foundation, we gave money in the hopes of doing good, but sometimes we gave simply because we were too busy to deal with the issues directly. Writing checks sometimes left an empty feeling, since we recognized that many of these social agencies receiving funds could not fix anything in a permanent way. Most social agencies administer relief—temporary relief at that. To solve issues in a more permanent way requires a much more devoted effort, which social services are not always able to deliver. We also knew that for people at risk of homelessness, becoming self-sustaining requires a transformational change often too daunting without a complex program and organization.

The Innovative Life Learning Center

We pondered this challenge for a long time—what is the solution, what is achievable? What could be or should be done to get people permanently onto their feet, and with dignity. Together we searched for a model and finally found the Homeless Center in South Bend, Indiana. I had heard they had a unique program to get local homeless people from where they were to the point where they could hold a job, and then to get a job. I invited five other people who I felt would be interested to fly with me to South Bend for a tour.

The people in South Bend were great! They were smart. There was an energy about the entire place that one could sense—people were walking fast. There was a sense of urgency. To me that is always a good sign. When people are smiling, walking fast, energized, it is because they are experiencing success.

Their program was a 24-week curriculum broken into four parts beginning with a six-week period named "Starting Over" and ending with another named

"Bravo." During Bravo, participants are taught how to get a job, how to keep a job, how to conduct oneself in the workplace, and how to interview, among other subjects. I was impressed, and our group returned home on the plane flying high—and not just in terms of altitude.

It took many years to get our own version of the South Bend educational approach into place, together with a big investment. Corporex owned an automobile dealership facility in Covington perfect for what we named the Life Learning Center. The location was dead center urban, those that would use our services could walk if necessary. But city officials fought us for years, preventing us from initiating the project. Finally, approximately 15 years ago, we opted to rent a small space and get started.

We began with just part of the curriculum we had developed, which was focused only on getting a job and was one week long. During this first course, we found a candidate to lead the effort named Denise Govan. She and Barbara Schaefer, the executive director of our family foundation, with the help of a consultant, began developing the curriculum. Today it is composed of both full-time and part-time sessions as part of a 12-week-long program leading to a "Certificate of Achievement." If a person completes the program and achieves the certificate we issue, one of our corporate employer-partners will likely offer that person a job.

After many years, an opportunity arose. The Commonwealth of Kentucky wanted to establish a career center where it could combine some of its social services into a shared facility. The City of Covington wanted to locate it in the dealership building we owned. The city also owned a separate building four blocks away, twice as large as our building but with three floors instead of one. That building was not a good fit for their purposes. So we made a deal with the city to trade buildings along with all the necessary permits to site the Life Learning Center's operations in building which they had acquired and specially zoned with an eye toward locating all community social services in one specially designated district.

Corporex contributed the dealership building to the Life Learning Center, and the Life Learning Center swapped buildings with the city. We then raised $2 million in retrofit funds, and created a beautiful facility with six classrooms, a computer lab, a 220-seat tiered gathering center, a restaurant, coffee shop, day care center, and provisions for a credit union. At about the same time, we sold a Five Seasons Sports facility in Cleveland. It had a huge fitness component, so we relocated the equipment and installed a beautiful fitness center at the Life Learning Center as part of the program. Fitness and wellness are part of the Life Learning Center's core curriculum and a crucial component of self-sustainability. We just recently partnered with St. Elizabeth Hospital to install what it styles a "Journey to Recovery" center on the top floor. St. Elizabeth will provide medical services as well as alcohol and drug counseling and psychiatric treatment.

The Life Learning Center is a success story with unlimited potential to change lives for the better. There are currently 100 volunteer faculty members who teach the curriculum, with another 100 volunteers who serve as what we call candidate support coordinators. Program participants are called candidates until they complete the curriculum and other qualification tests.

The parole boards found us soon after we opened for business. The U.S. penal system is such that when inmates complete their sentences, they are turned out on the street with no money and no experience. Felons are expected to be able to get a job and get back into society all on their own, despite having a record. Not much chance of that, so they end up back in prison. Today nearly 80 percent of our candidates are people with felony records looking for a path to life and stability. We started out to help the less hopeful and "at risk" members of our community, but at the Life Learning Center we have discovered an opportunity to help people now on the outside get back on their feet. Who is more at risk of homelessness than someone coming out of prison?!

Approximately five years after we launched the Life Learning Center with the abridged curriculum, a man who had gone through the program returned for an impromptu visit while a class was in session. He was invited to speak with the group, where he told his story. He shared how he had been imprisoned on a drug charge for more than five years. He reached into his wallet and pulled out a card he held up. "When I was released, I had this card," he said, showing his identification card, which, in addition to money for a cab or bus, is all they receive when they are released from prison. He told the class how he struggled to get work for one and a half years before finally stumbling upon the Life Learning Center, where he completed our one-week course called "Working for a Better Life." He told everyone how he got a job, then a promotion, then a better job, and another promotion. Then he raised his other hand and said, "And now I have this card." It was a Visa credit card.

There are so many stories about how people who have come to the center have landed jobs, learned to save money, got their driving privileges restored, and most importantly, been able to get custody of their children back and reunited their families. The results from the center show the kind of transformations that are possible.

Today the Life Learning Center is led by a unique individual—Alecia Webb-Edgington. Alecia's career began as a Kentucky state trooper. While a trooper, she rose through the ranks to Major and had 155 troopers reporting to her. She was the first Kentucky Homeland Security Secretary. She understands our clients, because her work as a state trooper and with the judicial system put her in touch with many good folks who for one reason or another violated the law or fell into poverty condition. She is disciplined and knowledgeable, and she is passionate about people and their success. She is the perfect person to be the CEO, and the center has progressed and expanded under her leadership.

The Samaritan Car Care Clinic

It might be hard to believe, but the number one inhibitor for people in poverty to get on their feet is transportation. If you do not have a car, you cannot get to work—you cannot even get to the interview to be considered for the job opening. Several years ago, the Life Learning Center began fixing up old bicycles. But we knew that wasn't enough.

From time to time, the Butler Foundation had been supporting the Madison Avenue Christian Church in Covington, which had a periodic clinic to repair cars when owners could not afford the cost. This small urban church was able to borrow a mechanic's garage every two to three months to repair cars all weekend. We asked the project leadership at Madison Avenue Christian Church if they would like to operate the car repair clinic full-time, rather than only on weekends. With their expression of interest, the Butler Foundation and Corporex together contributed a parcel of land and built a ground-up state-of-the-art repair facility with four bays. The R. C. Durr Foundation stepped up to match our investment, as it often partners with us and we with them. A total of seven automobiles could be worked on simultaneously in this brand-new facility.

So we now have a plan to initiate and fund a loan-to-own or rent-to-own financing program with creatively designed payment plans that will allow for modest payments in the first year then step up over time as the borrowers gain stability. The Samaritan Car Care Clinic enterprise will acquire and fix up automobiles to be redistributed. Both the financing as well as the car-repair program are methods by which we are attacking the problems of the less hopeful people in our region. The Life Learning Center's bicycle-refurbishing operation will be moved into this new facility and tripled in size.

Urban Community Developers, Inc.

Corporex recently established and has capitalized a not-for-profit corporation named Urban Community Developers to build infill housing on empty lots within urban areas. The purpose is not so much to create affordable housing but to raise the bar within neighborhoods and increase property values across the region. By building higher-end properties in empty lots, streets will be improved and surrounding neighbors perhaps inspired to invest in enhancing their own properties.

In one case, an entire city block consisting of twelve vacant lots has been acquired, and new homes will be built there to attract new residents. We will be building all of these homes simultaneously in order to create a model for change. This is another example of how a company can be more than a financial enterprise.

But there are myriad other ways the company and individual employees have strived to have a positive influence on our community. Those efforts often become public, as letters arrive from people who have benefited from some Corporex initiative or act of charity and feel called to write to express their gratitude. We are blessed to have these opportunities to give forward.

Part IV

Building Communities

"A corporation can be more than
a financial enterprise; and if it can be,
it should be."

—WILLIAM P. BUTLER

Chapter 16

Origins of Progress

To have left the place I grew up in, to have moved to a bigger city where there was a strong real estate economy and more available money, would have been the smartest business decision I could have made from a pure wealth perspective. But then again, I never pursued wealth for wealth's sake, personally or through my company. That is not to say I have not been a truly competitive business person. Success in business involves meeting the demands of our great free enterprise system.

If I Only Had $10,000

That said, I thought about money, and my lack thereof, a lot in the early days, when trying to finance the company was ridiculously difficult. I remember one evening in the early years while suffering with stress that I prayed to God, "If I only had $10,000, what I could do for You!" (One does not forget such earnest prayers.) Trying to build an enterprise like Corporex from scratch, in a third-tier population center, was, at best, a hard task. Being located in Covington, across from the big city and in a different state altogether, exacerbated the challenges we faced. The Cincinnati bankers in our early years of the 1960s and '70s looked upon real estate and real estate developers as too risky for lending. They also would not lend to a Covington-based firm because, as they recited, due to reciprocity arrangements, we should initiate the request with our "local" Covington banks. The divide was big, and still is in some respects, and the idea of bankers partnering was not a serious intent on either side of the river. The Covington banks were little and thought only about what their legal lending limits would allow. Packaging loans and participation was not common back then—not in this middle-American metro.

The largest loan we could get under the Covington banks' regulatory limitation was $450,000, and that did not begin to meet our needs. Finally, after 10 years in business, I met a high-level officer from First National Bank of Louisville and he offered to be our banker; he even extended the only line of credit we ever used, for $1 million. But First National of Louisville also extended us their maximum amount for commercial real estate development year after year: $15 million for speculative industrial building development. It was a great relationship for, say, 15 years, until National City out of Cleveland bought them. After that, it seemed like we were *persona non grata*, because at the time National City Bank was not focused on our line of work. They were more of a retail lender, and we were in commercial real estate development and construction. To National City, real estate development was too risky. Interestingly, National City failed and went out of business some 20 years later, during the 2008 financial meltdown, because they had bought a California-based mortgage lender who made real estate loans to the housing sector nationwide.

We travelled frequently in the '80s and '90s to New York City and Chicago, two financial centers, promoting our company and seeking loans for our projects. It was a difficult sell because, generally speaking, the big-city banks found Cincinnati (and especially Northern Kentucky) not very appealing for commercial development lending, again, due to its moderate growth rate. They viewed us as a slow-growth community and that added risk to their underwriting. Had I lived in Chicago, or Atlanta, or even Charlotte, it would have been different. In those cities, one could have lunch with a bank executive who may have immediate authority to loan $50 or $60 million for projects. One could develop a working relationship. I would not have had to travel around the country to the bigger cities, a time-consuming and inefficient means, and for the most part until later in the 1980s, those financial institutions were of no help to us.

Simply put, places where growth is more accelerated attract financial investments, they appeal to investment sources with money to lend and a desire to do so. This allows more small businesses to be more financeable and to grow more quickly and successfully. To some extent this stigma prevails even now 40 to 50 years later. Growth is essential to attracting investment support.

If we had had larger banks or if we had been a unified metropolitan center, these hurdles would not have plagued us. More money could have been available on the Kentucky side and more small businesses like ours at the time could have grown faster and with less risk.

It would also have been a lot easier had I just moved across the river to Cincinnati and become a part of the Cincinnati scene early in my career. A number of Northern Kentucky entrepreneurs chose to do just that, but that never tempted me as much because of a sense of loyalty and maybe even duty to the place where I grew up.

Even though I did not relocate to Cincinnati, I have enjoyed many strong business relationships with most of the CEOs of the many corporations headquartered there, community organization executives as well. Many of those relationships have grown into deep personal friendships for Sue and me. Those who have befriended me and Corporex are generally those who are like-minded about a commitment to service for those in need, and like-minded about viewing the entire SMA as one resource, one place. Greater Cincinnati, including Northern Kentucky, is blessed to be home to many leaders who have a strong sense of community, and the will to serve and to give.

I have met them through the United Way, the Boy Scouts, chambers of commerce, and other charitable and community-focused movements. I was honored to be the first Northern Kentucky businessman asked onto the board of the Greater Cincinnati Chamber of Commerce. Corporex developed some notable buildings in Cincinnati as well and were accepted on many fronts, and our commitment to the bigger picture did not go unnoticed. The highest recognition given in Cincinnati is to be designated a "Great Living Cincinnatian."

The title speaks for itself, and as a Northern Kentucky citizen, I was so honored in 2017 with that award. I consider this award and another, the "Carl H. Lindner Award for Entrepreneurial and Civic Spirit," to be among the best of my career

But in the end, I am pleased that we resolved to stay rooted in Northern Kentucky. My overarching goal now is to have Corporex remain domiciled in Northern Kentucky for years to come; moreover, that the executives who lead it shall remain committed to our corporate culture of service and contribution—to continue to make a difference here.

Again, I found myself in a business that was important to community progress. Northern Kentucky was and remains my apostolate of sorts, and it was and remains my responsibility to answer the call so to speak—to make a difference in this smaller population center.

At Corporex, we have tried in many ways to support progress, and with some success. Until recently, we were most noted for having developed the vacant riverfront beginning in the mid-1980s, adding tall office buildings and hotels. As the developer of Rivercenter, we were instrumental in getting Governor Brereton Jones to pass legislation for a convention center. He even convened a special session of legislature where our facility was one of only two items on the agenda for the entire state because, as he told me, "I made you a promise." In Northern Kentucky alone we developed three industrial parks. We pioneered the first indoor tennis facility and then tripled its size. I became a pretty good tennis player but, as I joked in 1971, "We people of Northern Kentucky first had to learn how to hold the racquet."

In addition to the first high-rise office building, Corporex developed the one-of-a-kind world-class Ascent high-rise condominiums and another very unique project, Domaine de la Rive. Domaine de la Rive, as it turns out, was the breakthrough property and defined a critical pivot point leading to our community's unfolding future. We proved for the very first time that people of means who had been Cincinnati residents for years would cross that river to Kentucky for the highest-quality homes in the urban sector, especially when they reached the age and desire to downsize or to return to the urban setting where many of us grew up.

The Face of the Community Will Be Forever Changed by Our Catalytic Developments

Domaine de la Rive was truly an extremely high-risk, pioneering engagement that, looking back, has paved the way for the entire Northern Kentucky urban center to achieve high-end residential developments not seen in this community. It has served to shape the future of the area, in ways not yet known or understood. There were only 11 condominiums in Domaine de la Rive, but that was sufficient to be the pilot for the next big project that followed five years later, the Ascent, a neighboring 25-story structure with seven times the number of residential units. Additional multistory condominium projects quickly followed in Newport and Bellevue, on the river. Other such high-end residential projects are being planned in current times by multiple residential developers, made possible solely by our having established price points on sales of our units that are even higher than on the more developed Cincinnati side of the river. We were able to demonstrate repeatedly that buyers would pay up for residences of quality design, and on the higher end of the spectrum of housing without regard for geographic or political location. That has made all the difference. Indeed Domaine De La Rive and the Ascent projects are the pivotal acts that will have shaped the Northern Kentucky urban fabric. And it seems safe to forecast that 20 or 30 years into the future, the entire appearance, the skyline as well as perceptions of Northern Kentucky, will be dramatically enhanced because we undertook these original pioneering risks, and succeeded, albeit with a lot of patience.

In the course of writing, I was reminded of an experience from over 40 years ago, which I had completely forgotten until now. But it is etched in my mind and worth sharing because it helps to understand the potential future.

I was touring the city of Düsseldorf, which was fully developed on both banks of the river Rhine in Germany. This European city is not unlike Greater Cincinnati in many ways. I have never lost the picture in my mind about the way Düsseldorf had been developed, which must have been because of a "noble, logical diagram," as Daniel Burnham would put it—a well-planned vision.

The buildings were consistent in height and color, modern—even with age. On the west bank of the river are series of architecturally attractive mid-rise and high-rise residential buildings. In my mind that was the potential future of Covington and Newport. On the east bank are the commercial high-rise buildings, again, very attractively designed. It was impressive how it all appeared and came together, and I automatically associated this picture with the long-term development potential for our two river communities of Cincinnati and Northern Kentucky—I witnessed what could be!

In the late 1970s, Cincinnati had not undertaken any redevelopment of the produce district by the river. There were no parks and not yet the stadiums. Indeed, I think the Düsseldorf picture has been alive in my subconscious lo these many years because while Northern Kentucky will have more than residential type developments, the south banks of our river are developing into a largely upper-class living sector in the whole region. To comprehend this picture in full, one must try to project the rate of investment in such residential developments forward from the number of projects that have already occurred in, say just the past 15 years. And then project the prospects for increased numbers of living units that will likely occur. It will accelerate. The Corporex Ovation! development will, in itself, include 1,000 high-quality residential homes and apartments.

When enough people move to these future buildings, shops and retail stores will open anew, and the urban population outflow will be reversed. This is what lies ahead for the Northern Kentucky urban sector, and my hope is that we get out front in ways to both stimulate this revival, and to manage its quality and appearance.

Although these are visions of what could be, we do know this: such socio-economic advances will not be by accident, but rather by planning, design and risk-taking—acts essential to pressing the community forward. The more risk-takers there are, the more growth we will achieve. The more growth we achieve, the more risk-takers will be attracted to develop—and more abundant progress will be experienced.

On the non-residential side, by developing the Towers of Rivercenter, Corporex was able to lure corporate headquarters to Covington, which was devoid of any significant corporate headquarters for national companies. At one point, the Towers of Rivercenter housed seven distinct national/international or publicly traded corporate headquarters—another breakthrough.

In the suburbs, at CirclePort business park, we made similar strides, ultimately luring Toyota North American headquarters, Citicorp, General Electric, Johnson Controls, The Gap, State Farm Insurance, Wild Flavors from Germany, and others to our community's fabric. Shortly after construction of the first Rivercenter tower, a coalition of CEOs evenly balanced between Ohio and Kentucky companies, founded the Metropolitan Club on the top level with the theme "Bridge the Bridges." This was then a stunning example of what can occur with a joint working relationship, representing the combined resources of both Cincinnati and Northern Kentucky leadership. The Metropolitan Club has been a valuable asset that has served to bring both the Northern Kentucky citizenry and Cincinnati leaders closer together. The challenge today is forging a similar level of partnering to move the entire region forward at an accelerated pace.

Development Takes on Multiple Forms

Until 2015, Northern Kentucky had no community-wide public charity organization. Cincinnati had the Greater Cincinnati Foundation, and Louisville founded the Greater Louisville Foundation even before that. In Northern Kentucky, we badly needed a vehicle for our citizens to be able to initiate charitable accounts and unite to make group gifts to make a larger impact. Most recently, four like-minded leaders in Northern Kentucky partnered to change that:, Bob Zapp, Chuck Scheper, Will Ziegler, and I. We were quickly joined by a blue-chip group of executives to form the Horizon Community Funds of Northern Kentucky. All of us wish this had happened a good 35 years earlier.

The Horizon Community Funds promises to be a powerful vehicle supporting diverse programs affecting quality of life, as well as being a meaningful fuel for unifying the people through community giving, sharing, and service. Horizons Community Funds quickly adopted a bold, overarching goal for Northern Kentucky as a whole: to become known, as "The Giving Community."

I do not make these recitations out of pride or to brag about Corporex. However, these events and projects are necessary parts of the story that plays out in these chapters, especially our community's future. All of these physical development projects, as well as the organizations formed, are ingredients in a recipe for the future. The goal is for more people to understand the historical components of progress, the legs of the table so to speak, as key to accelerating advancement of the larger community. Indeed, there has been progress and growth already, and it is also very clear that many undertakings could not have been accomplished alone. We know that. Milestones are achieved when acting jointly and cooperatively. That is what community is all about!

Chapter 17

The Case for Change

Corporex as a company and I as an individual have always been unapologetic advocates for major change.

Notwithstanding my commitment to bettering our region, there has been pushback from critics for some reason. I think they do not understand me or my makeup. Being often referred to as a visionary, I see the future and what could be—then I also see the current state of affairs on the issues, and the hurdles in between that must be overcome to achieve progress. Couple that clear vision of what is possible with the can-do attitude of an entrepreneur with deep conviction and sense of purpose and you have a formula for impatience, as well as for progress. However, when others do not share those same observations, varying perceptions give rise to misunderstanding and division, creating barriers to progress. But without vision and impatience, there will be little progress.

George Bernard Shaw was famously known for his statement: "The reasonable man adapts himself to the world; the unreasonable one persists in trying to adapt the world to himself. Therefore, all progress depends on the unreasonable man." I am comfortable being known as an unreasonable man if it leads to progress.

The earlier example about how one man, Daniel Burnham, the architect and land planner, made all the difference in shaping the Chicago shoreline and skyline, is evidence enough that to constructively plan and paint pictures is essential and correct—even expected of some of us. When speaking about Greater Cincinnati, Duke University professor Michael Gallis remarked: "I see the remnants of a once-great city, and I struggle to find the resolve to make it great again." Then he went on to suggest that there needs to be a revival of a will to change—an essential to compete within an economy which has become globalized. In our Northern Kentucky sector, as mentioned earlier, this is our challenge, while at the same time working to reverse 200 years of history. These are not insignificant slopes to mount—but wonderful challenges that will ultimately require all the people to act as one. A long time ago, Mark Twain is reputed to have said: "When I die, I want to be in Cincinnati—everything happens much later there." That label, that culture, may or may not be earned, but it exists and prevails. The label encompasses Northern Kentucky as well, because we are part of the official Cincinnati metropolitan statistical area.

Those of us who were born and raised here are proud to be where we are. In particular, we are especially boastful of the strong value system inherent in this population center. Greater Cincinnati and Northern Kentucky are together known as a good place to raise children. Having traveled extensively, I've come to know many great cities, each with their own strengths. And I came to the conclusion that what makes our Cincinnati/Northern Kentucky community special is that people can form deep personal relationships quickly. They can, and do, regularly share their lives over a kitchen table. They build levels of trust with others that is rare in larger and faster paced metropolitan areas. It is something unique to our DNA, and it is valuable. It is special.

Yet as an entrepreneur in the commercial development business, I cannot help but be frustrated and impatient with the progress being made to improve the quality of life here, and to create more opportunities for local growth. We must overcome those elements that give rise to a fragmented culture in order to hold our ground in a globalized world order.

The primary cause of our fractured community is rooted in our political and cultural fragmentation. Three states intersect but do not join together otherwise. Because of that, there is less excitement in and about our overall region. The term for that in economic circles is "low energy." Whatever it is called, the lack of progress and excitement drives many younger professionals to settle in more dynamic centers.

We need to change that, too.

This lack of younger talent causes a domino effect because where younger people want to live, so must corporations locate because they need those brains and bodies. The only way to overcome our perceived deficiency regarding quality growth for the region is to pool our resources: financial and social. To do so would tell the wider world that we are a unified place, to show that we are one homogenous center—that growth and opportunity and excitement can be found here. We need to become proactive in changing the perception. It is a monumental challenge, the solution to which has escaped us to date.

This hurdle is not necessarily unique to us. Kansas City, Missouri, and Kansas City, Kansas, and Minneapolis and Saint Paul seem to have progressed as one. Metro New York and northern New Jersey came together to form the New York Port Authority and other cross-state actions. Our situation may even be a little more challenging, given there are three states involved, but if we could somehow begin with the core, Cincinnati and Northern Kentucky, get a point of beginning, maybe the rest would fall into place—and sooner than we might anticipate.

A Noble, Logical Diagram, Once Recorded

In our case, a series of major joint operating projects involving both Cincinnati and Northern Kentucky will be needed to paint a picture of a place on the move. These projects must be highly visible and symbolic in scope and nature. The elevated loop rail concept mentioned earlier from the Quest vision publication of the late '90s would be effective both visually and logistically, but yet feasibly wrap the urban cities in a symbolically unifying way. This one initiative could have far-reaching benefits, both to bring the diverse forces together and to change the entire environment of the wider community.

Just think of the impact. Consider the picture of progress this highly visual and symbolic contemporary monorail addition would create. Such a contemporary feature wrapping elements on both sides of the river, connecting two states, would convey to the world community a perception of cooperation, moreover of unity, wholeness, and progressiveness, too. A perception of progressiveness would be the change that gives rise to the excitement we seek. This singular endeavor would be a major marketing benefit for the entire 360-degree region, and could also accelerate the activities of developments for urban living in all the cities along the river. If this is not the best action for the entire region another cross-state project must be found. Otherwise, we will suffer the fate of other northern geographic centers that have lost appeal, lost corporate headquartered enterprises completely, and the higher paying job opportunities and people that go with them.

A similar, if not the same challenge, that faces Greater Cincinnati as a region exists within our smaller-population sector of Northern Kentucky. Namely, multiple, separate political jurisdictions and multiple municipalities. But with one big exception! We are smaller in size. There are bonds among us as well as a recognition of this sector's dilemma. To that end, we should be able to get our arms around the issues and see the goal more clearly. We should also be able to get results more quickly.

We have not just recently come to the recognition of the problem. A group of the entrepreneurial leaders with whom I worked back in the 1970s, often found ourselves meeting over this very subject. We met almost weekly at the Drawbridge Hotel. I do not remember all who attended, but Gerry Deters, the Drawbridge's owner, was there, and I would suggest was the convener. Gerry, now deceased, understood. He and I spent many hours discussing one-on-one and also in such meetings, how we felt about our community and ourselves as citizens, due to how people in Cincinnati looked upon us. Bob Aldemeyer, the County Judge Executive, was always at those gatherings. Frank Sommerkamp from Cincinnati Bell was usually there. Ken Harper, and Clyde Middleton when a state representative, I think Ralph Drees occasionally, Gordon Martin for sure, and others were at those get-togethers. A few drinks would always loosen the conversation, but the topic invariably centered on what we each felt strongly about ourselves, about our community and what could we do to change for the better. Eventually, it did lead to some measure of change.

I recall clearly that in our early gatherings, we all shared very low self-esteem about who we were as residents of Northern Kentucky. In part, these meetings led to the first visioning exercise to determine who we wanted to be and how to get there. When John Y. Brown Jr. became governor in 1980, he commissioned the "Governors Economic Development Task Force," which was simply the trigger, the catalyst, we needed, and a framework for action. He provided the charge: an opportunity to act, to do something, an expectation set by him. That first visioning project 40 years ago identified "disunity and fragmentation" as the overwhelming inhibitor to the community's progress and the cause for its low self-esteem. And yet, while we have made measurable progress in a number of economic development sectors, 40 years later we are still talking about unity and consolidation as being a far-away concept. This is not to say that there has not been any progress overcoming fragmentation—there has been, but not much. If our underlying purpose as leaders and citizens is to serve the people, why have we not solved this issue? What is it that escapes us as leaders?

The Heartbeat of the Urban Core

The Latin word for heart is cor. No human can have vitality without a vibrant heart. It is the same for our community of 400,000 people, lately being referred to as "One NKY." One NKY's "cor," its heart, its urban center, must be vibrant. I'm excited and engaged by the possibilities I see here, even as I cross my 80th birthday.

Why did the pioneers in America, those who first floated down our local Ohio River and settled on the shores, not stake out large tracts of land for each to own, so they could live on their large estates? Why did they instead build cities—Covington, Newport, Cincinnati—living on small parcels of land mostly 25 feet wide? The answer is simple, of course. We needed each other. We need each other for practical objectives, infrastructure, utilities, services, necessities that cause us to unite, to work together. And that need, albeit somewhat differently described given our evolution, will always be there for us to respond to. But we also need each other for quality of life, protection, support personally, to enjoy day to day, to share our lives, and to grow as people.

We the people thrive when we are in unity, especially when we are united for an overarching goal. Marriage thrives where there is true unity. Businesses achieve more when there is unity within its culture. Partnerships can give rise to exponential outcomes. Unity is a big word to me—a big love word again.

A Name to Call Our Own

A huge hurdle threatening our future prospects in the Northern Kentucky sector is the reality that our population is deprived of an identity: a single name identity, a name to call our own, one that speaks to community oneness and generates pride. We in this population center are referenced only to a place on a map called Northern Kentucky, we are known only by our location. We are three counties consisting of more than 25 municipalities, each with its individual name. We lack one holistic name identity for the region; this is a glaring disadvantage that everyone recognizes but has not to date had the collective will to correct, perhaps because the challenge seems daunting. It will take time, patience, and perseverance, but we must simply begin using a well-constructed educational process. Our One NKY population must be educated about the importance of a name to call our own, about which we will rally. We have much to be proud of that goes unrecognized due to our splintered personality—and of course one can readily relate the drag on our progress inherent in this deficiency.

When my wife, Sue, and I travel and find ourselves in other parts of the country, we are inevitably asked where Corporex is based. I tend to say, almost automatically, "Cincinnati," and then explain, "Well, actually in Kentucky, across the river." It is just too cumbersome to respond "Covington" or "Fort Mitchell," or "Newport," or "Florence, in Kentucky." No one knows where that is. Having to explain exactly in relation to a named city is a bit embarrassing. But folks do know where Louisville is, and even Lexington and Ashland, which are smaller. And they know where Cincinnati is.

I am not comfortable with this condition and wish we as a community would develop the resolve to fix this. Now. What will it take to get one name that the 400,000+ residents of this area could claim and proclaim? How much more difficult will it be to accomplish when we are no longer 400,000 but rather 600,000 or 700,000 people that are referred to as only a geographical location on a map?

The Advent of One NKY as a Place

There is reason to be optimistic about the new alliance of CEOs formed in recent years by top executives who share some mutual concern, with a desire to make a difference where other organizations have not. This organization began as a small tight unit of CEOs who shared a desire to act, and expressed the courage to follow through. "Bold Change" is the theme, perhaps the mission, these 20 CEOs have adopted. In recent months within that group the term "One NKY" was invented, and the organization's name changed to One NKY Alliance. That phrase in itself will make a difference if fostered over a sustained period. This mantra will hopefully be used widely: on billboards, on agencies, and talked about in headlines. It may take 10 or 20 years to get across the message to enough of the citizenry, but the term One NKY, if used intensely, will make a difference. It is a step—not just a small step. We have a start. Sometimes big steps do not require big money but carry a big message.

One NKY Alliance has launched a project to develop a state-of-the-art headquarters building in which the so called "growth" organizations will be housed. It will be a stunning, visual symbol of unity and cooperation on the part of the private sector, an example that will hopefully be observed for its significance by the public and governmental sector, too. One NKY Alliance; the Northern Kentucky Chamber of Commerce; Meet Northern Kentucky, the hotel and tourism organization; Tri-Ed, the combined three county economic growth agency; Horizons Community Funds, the recently incorporated public charity; and the Catalytic Development Fund organizations will all be housed in this new building and share the cost savings and otherwise unaffordable high-tech space. All of these organizations have one thing in common—growth of the community. To bring the growth agencies under one roof has been one of the projects from the earliest vision reports; and the CEOs decided that the Alliance could not effectively suggest consolidation governments when the private sector had not yet succeeded. The One NKY headquarters building will be symbolic to that end.

The term "One NKY" itself is a big message in a very simple, understandable, and visual form. Maybe someday the population center itself will be known simply as "One NKY"—the place, instead of Northern Kentucky, the reference to a location on a map. Sounds unorthodox, but that could be the name of the place. One NKY. Or maybe Ovation!, an approach similar to the style of Celebration, a new city Disney developed in Florida. Neither, of course, may in the end be the selected name and may not be the best, but, well, like my mom always said, "Put it in your pipe and smoke it." Let's at least consider it. To change the reference from Northern Kentucky to One NKY does not require legislation or a vote of the people.

There's Power Within a Shared Vision

I have searched for the cause of inaction and sense that what escapes us, what is blocking our progress currently, is that there is no one clear picture for what could be, what should be, in the minds of those to whom the challenge for change and progress falls. We need a well-defined picture—a mutually constructed and understood concept for the future of this One NKY community. The same is lacking with regard to the larger Greater Cincinnati region, and the so-called 360-degree community will not come about without a mutually constructed concept that escapes all. I have named it the elusive shared vision.

At the moment, there is no mutually comprehensive agreement regarding where it is we desire to go, how to get there, or what the future looks like when we get there—at least not one we can point to. It has been said, "If you cannot see it, you cannot shoot it." At the moment, there is no clear vision of what we actually want to be as a total One NKY community. The vision studies of 1981,

1997, and the one called Vision 2015, tried to paint a picture of what could be, and to develop a blueprint to achieve the picture that the authors tried to describe in each. Each effort helped to create goals but did not in itself succeed in forming a sustainable shared vision.

The most effective report with respect to outcomes, was the most simplified version, called Northern Kentucky's Future, which was published in 1981. While it was not intended to be the entire solution at the time, it did help to bring leadership together around a cause. It proved what could happen with a shared vision. Substantial progress was made for the 15 to 20 years that followed. But neither that publication, nor the second process called Quest, were intended to be the roadmap to the ultimate goal for a total community with consolidated services, a unified population center, and, finally, with a name to call its own. To get there will take much more collective will of the kind not often witnessed.

There are benchmark examples of the power within a true shared vision worth our attention. The most impressive example is manifested by the founding fathers of our country.

The leaders who came together to frame the U.S. Constitution clearly demonstrated what can occur by acting together and with a clear goal and common purpose. Indeed, they had a collective agreement about who and what they wanted to be and to achieve. Those brave souls found a way to solve the problem of the time. No doubt the feelings were deep and the debate likely aggressive and emphatic, but they came together and they forged ONE United States from a loose confederation of states. Sound familiar? This could not have been achieved had those folks not shared a common vision that was worth fighting for.

But we need not look beyond our own local community for examples of that same level of courage. Recall that Newport had a terrible reputation. As they said, "it was wide open" and controlled by the mob. There are multiple books written about the so-called mob, the syndicate out of Cleveland that owned the gambling houses and bars, and bribed the officials to look away. And this prevailed for decades.

But in the mid-1960s, the community leaders there banded together to take decisive action that heretofore they had been unwilling to bring themselves to do. They formed what was known as the Committee of 500, and they elected George Ratterman to become county sheriff to enforce the law. They went up against the mob—think about that! Consider the incredible courage they mustered for the sake of their hometown. It was not easy, for certain, as the mob fought back with dirty tactics. They were not about to let a group of citizens ruin their money machines. But in this event, the citizenry had developed a collective vision about the future they wanted, about how they wanted to be perceived, and about their children's futures. In other words, they developed a shared vision, a collective vision, and that vision energized the leaders and the followers too—and they succeeded in what would otherwise seem an impossible goal against such incredible odds. No, we do not have to look beyond for examples, for courage and foresight.

I do know this. Were it not for the shared vision of the business and professional leaders of the 1950s and 1960s who formed the Committee of 500 and stood firm for their community, the way we people view ourselves in the 2020s would be with much more embarrassment than pride. To take on the mob took courage, determination, and most essentially, a shared vision worth the risks. While we in One NKY have not yet formed a united place, the progress we have, in fact, made would not have been possible were it not for the Committee of 500 who banded together much like the founders of our country to create the foundation on which we currently operate and wish to improve via further change. Theirs was indeed bold and courageous action, bold change.

To most of the leadership who were not corrupted back then, the problem appeared insurmountable. To others, it was not a choice but a duty. Those who undertook the cleanup of the Newport, especially, but Covington too, are models of what can be accomplished despite overwhelming odds.

Again, those who framed the Constitution found that the purpose was greater than the relationships with the complacent people of the time. Those who formed the Committee of 500 in Campbell County had to decide that they would be willing to sacrifice somewhere in order to do what was right for the community at large. What they were doing was for the very long-term future—for future generations to come. I appreciate what they did, as I cannot imagine this place today had they not stood up.

It seems to me this level of commitment is expected of those of us who find ourselves in positions of leadership within communities. It is expected of those of us who are gifted with skills and success.

Chapter 18

Change Is a Team Sport

I have always been a big believer in the power of partnerships. When people come together in a true partner relationship, two plus two equals five, not four, just as five plus five can become 20, and 10 plus 10 can be 50. The results are magnified. No mountain is too big to scale, no river too wide—not even the Ohio that separates Cincinnati from Northern Kentucky.

I also know that there is no bridging the bridges between Cincinnati and our Northern Kentucky population centers so long as we in Kentucky allow ourselves to remain fragmented, splintered by political jurisdictions and other less defined cultural and power centered forces. We cannot allow politicians with limited vision and courage to run our municipalities. We simply must find a way to combine multiple limited financial resources to magnify our impact. We will be in a strong position to address the 360-degree metropolitan area when we in Northern Kentucky are looked upon with respect for being managed in an effective way and for being unified. One NKY must become a reality; forces of economics will cause it "someday" if we fail to bring it all together in a proactive way. To effect such change is, in my view, our responsibility. This is the responsibility that comes with being successful, being leaders. Such change dynamic, such progress over time has always fallen upon the non-elected leadership to design, to lead the charge, to set the pace. Only then can elected officials facilitate the will of the community.

We often find ourselves in conversations where we tend to compare ourselves to high-growth areas of the country, like Austin. They ask: "Why can't we be like Austin?" And my response is: "We do not want to be like Austin or any other place, necessarily. We want to be One NKY in the form and substance that we are privileged to shape." It is our determination to do—or to continue to kick the can down the road.

Our One NKY community has inherent strengths upon which we should capitalize. In many ways, we are a true community. We support each other. We have a personality that is actually less competitive than many population centers. We have natural resources, the river, relatively lower taxes, the Greater Cincinnati/Northern Kentucky International Airport. We benefit from the sports and museums, art and cultural components of our sister community to the north.

And yet we need to find the will, the determination to take the big step, construct the shared vision, define the goals, and execute in a collective and unified manner. It cannot be done alone, or by any small number of people, nor would that be energizing or rewarding. The reward is found in doing it shoulder to shoulder, in a team-spirited way, collectively.

Working together, we can leverage Northern Kentucky's greatest assets and heighten its visibility in order to attract more attention, more residents, and more opportunity. We need to take that other road in the wood and see where it takes us. That will make all the difference.

Overarching Motivation

People sometimes wonder and, if they do not know us, they may even speculate about our intentions regarding the risky projects for which Corporex has been occasionally known. This is especially true with regard to developments of all kinds in our hometown. Our competitors, as well as others in the financial sectors of banking, have sometimes criticized us and questioned our judgment for undertaking what otherwise is known as extremely high-risk pioneering. Indeed, in our urban sector, Corporex has taken and continues to take outsized risks but for transformative-level developments. We do not undertake such high-risk endeavors in cities other than our own, nor do we go looking for higher-risk opportunities. But when a project emerges that would have a transformative effect on the area, we are likely to at least explore it. We adhere to the tried-and-true analytics for such developments, but in our home base we have done so with a commitment of a higher order—for the long-term community progress, indeed, as another way that a corporate enterprise delivers more than financial gains to its shareholders, delivers contribution to its surroundings.

Moreover, developers of buildings and business parks and subdivisions are unique in terms of the impact their products—that is, their developments—if well done, can make on the community. This is especially true for development of larger commercial properties. At Corporex, we have observed the high-rise buildings we have built on the river are a source of pride for all the citizens about the place where they live. We frequently observe people looking up at the buildings within Rivercenter, especially the Ascent, and pointing. Indeed, buildings can become like standard-bearers that people look to and are uplifted by. To the extent those standards are leading-edge designs of the highest quality, the population actually experiences a lift. High-quality architecture is essential to these ends. Although expensive, it adds significantly to the surrounding environment and contributes to progress in the course of its positive impact on the population.

Sourcing the Fuel for Change

Corporex expanded into faster-growing cities and has built and developed in 27 states to date, and, in so doing, learned from more progressive cities. Involvement in high-growth cities made it possible to generate money faster than could be accomplished in our slower local economy. And with less risk. The properties we developed in those regions generally proved more profitable. Now we have been able to come home with that money and are leveraging what we learned and what we earned with increased scale. Our national outreach has also helped to expand funds set aside for charitable and social purposes that will make a long-term impact. Going national not only expanded our knowledge and mindset, but helped us to build up the financial resources to honor our early life commitments—to give and to serve in the place where we were formed. The current $1 billion-plus Ovation! project is just such an example. It involves a huge up-front capital investment to build the raised platform for what will become a model living, working, and entertainment center. Ovation! will once again change the skyline and perception of the Northern Kentucky population center for the next 100 years and be a catalyst for future investments on many fronts and types. The just-completed, state-of-the-art MegaCorp indoor/outdoor music pavilion is another example of what could be.

Yes, real estate development is a great business, if for no other reason than for the side benefit of knowing that what we build as developers will impact generations to come. If Corporex were a manufacturer, we would put the product on the shipping dock and never see it again. In our case, we enjoy our product, we are reminded constantly of our mission and purpose, and rewarded for doing it with extra care. This is all in keeping with the culture we have developed and evolved at Corporex over our 55-plus years of enterprise building.

The Only Thing We Take with Us When We Depart This Life Is What We Gave Away

Orienting the company to the sense of community contribution has been personally rewarding as a private entrepreneur, but rewarding also for the many employees of Corporex, who recognize that their work contributed to making a long-term difference and, in turn, benefitted the very poorest among our citizenry. I have sensed that this element of our culture gives rise to an energy, a spirit, to do more. I struggle to comprehend why more organizations do not highlight community contribution in their written statement of purpose—because it is satisfying and adds a deeper sense of purpose to the workplace.

In my case, again, this commitment stems from a deep spiritual belief. The essence of my belief is that we are here on this planet, living this life, for the sole purpose of spiritual growth in quest of the next life, or the life to which we will return. In either case, when we do exit, all the material elements of this life are for naught, worthless—except for what outreach, what service we rendered with our resources while here. Too much money left behind in estates has a reputation for destroying the generations that are intended to benefit from our hard work. We run the risk of depriving our children of their opportunity to grow from within, a by-product of working for success, building something—indeed, building ourselves from within, spiritually.

Spiritual growth, I have discerned, is a love-rooted phenomenon. Piety is something else. Love is the key, the substance of spirituality and thus spiritual growth. My own study, learning and listening through the years suggests that to grow spiritually is to grow in love dimensionally. The more we grow spiritually by giving, the more we grow in love and in our capacity to share. That is what I believe, almost quantitatively. I guess such is my engineering orientation. To grow spiritually is to move in the direction of the Source, the Light, the one we call God. I am pretty sure I got a glimpse of that light back when I was 21 and had my special encounter.

These are the convictions I have come to. This is why the word "community" is so important to me. Building community to me is to grow in union with others—to grow in a shared way, which to me is the preferred way. For me, personal growth occurs through the process of serving, especially serving those whose path in life is more difficult or whose hopes are more limited. When we build or contribute to our community, we provide more opportunity for the less hopeful to advance out of their current social place, to a more wholesome place. When we do it together, well, that is more fulfilling, much more rewarding for all. Fun! We become more unified. In a fully performing community, people become bonded, and no one would deny that when we feel a bond, we feel loved. I believe this with my whole heart. In actuality, I know this reality full well: "The only thing we take with us when we leave this life is what we gave away while we were here." In other words, we take with us what is our heart, the depths of soul, our developed state. That is what goes with us into the next realm and determines our happiness or unhappiness, our unrest or our peacefulness in the next life.

The non-believer is so unfortunately harmed in this regard. But for the believer, it is mandatory to seek out service, and sharing, and supporting, and giving generously. I know this: I have never felt true love more than when I sensed my own feelings after having given something of significant value to someone who needed it more than me. It is an interesting exercise, which allows us to fully experience in a tangible way that force we call love; that four-letter word comes alive. Therein lies the proof, first hand, that in giving we receive. In other words, in giving we grow.

I am a believer. In fact, I have changed my language from "I believe" to "I know." Too many events have occurred in my life—callings, so to speak, or interventions—for me not to accept these learnings as reality. I am confident about these conclusions, based not only on faith, but on study, from discernment, listening, and more so from the special encounters, the callings, the multiple crises, too, and multiple personal failures that I have experienced and dealt with throughout my corporate and personal career. Each has its lesson and each lesson is an opportunity to connect with the higher powers, whether internal or else. We just have to bring ourselves to be open to the possibilities.

Which brings me back to the term community and its importance to our lives. The two components of the word mean "unity in common" such has always been essential to life, and deserves to be foremost in our minds, a responsibility we all share.

Chapter 19

Next Chapters

My wish is that I never lose the capacity for new dreams, new visions. What a great ride it has been, as Sue coined, "dreaming dreams and following them." Such is an exciting life experience. But I sense it is not the end. There is more to do in answering the calls, but also in responding to what has been built, and to position that foundation for future horizons, and opportunities for those associates who have come into my world and who seek to achieve success with a sense of purpose.

I have studied companies that have reached greatness, like those described in Jim Collins's book *Good to Great.* Such level of achievement does not happen overnight. In Cincinnati there is Procter & Gamble, a great company, now more than 185 years in business. Then there is Kroger corporation, too. I have wondered what those companies were like when they were like us, 50-plus years in existence. I think the first 50 years are best understood as the foundation, the platform on which the future is built, but at a continuously accelerated rate of progress.

This analogy allows one to benchmark and to project forward about the possibilities of the future for Corporex and its future leadership, and for the communities and people it will serve. I never believed in goals that were too well-defined as to be limiting. They have a way of becoming barriers. For example, when a young person states that his or her goal is to be a millionaire before age 35 or 40 but gets there much sooner and then unconsciously backs down, that person inadvertently shot himself or herself in the foot. I think there are no limits, only aspirations without limit by which we should guide ourselves, and the same goes for the total community in which we live and serve.

Now with the opportunity to look over the experience of building the business, I find myself somewhat critical of my efforts. I see all the ways Corporex could have been better, how I could have staffed it differently with an eye more to building the business for self-sufficiency. I have accused myself of building developments, and people, and communities, rather than building a business. I am not speaking of the financial strength. I do not doubt that every guy like me, every entrepreneur who has built a business, has similar thoughts later in life. But what I see is the Corporex name that is known nationally for quality, for integrity, for innovation, for contribution—and, well, one could justly conclude such is success defined. There is incredible value in the Corporex reputation—priceless in many ways because such foundations cannot be purchased for any amount of money. It can only be due to the many days and nights of work, struggle, resolve, commitment, and, yes, the dreams—the dreams!

Follow your dreams. Do not be afraid to dream, to aim high, without limits, and to suffer, if necessary, because you stretched as a result of your reaching for accomplishment, especially when accomplishment is born out of a desire to serve, to give back in the end—as we did along the way. The reward inherent to that is what makes all the difference. It is hard to explain, to share the magnitude of the reward in doing for the higher order. One must live it, earn it so to speak, to comprehend.

Focusing on the challenges, the difficulties, the multiple recessions as author has allowed me to relate substantive lessons learned, what I consider to be experiences worth sharing, though they may overshadow the more positive experiences of our corporate career. For sure, there were many highlights and victories, events in which we celebrated and enjoyed our achievements, and those could double the length of this book at the expense of passing over a message most worthy—about a dimension worth sharing, that is about the challenges that had to be overcome, about mission and purpose, about courage, and culture, and, well, growth in all its dimensions that comes forth in the course of the journey.

In retrospect, it seems to me the truly good times, the larger causes for celebration, are not found so much in occasional events or milestones along the way, but more in the overarching outcomes that have resulted from building an enterprise like Corporex over these many years.

The successes Corporex has achieved involving people, growth, developments, and service to the community, cumulatively serve to magnify our individual efforts. In the end, all the hard work, all the challenges, stress, and difficulties overcome have resulted in a corporate platform with the capability to change communities, to improve lives. What could be more worthy of celebration?

The best outcome is found in the growth that all of us who have been involved in the evolution of Corporex have personally experienced. And it is so—"all growth happens out of difficulty." What is good is the heightened inner sense of fulfillment that we, and I in particular, are privileged to actually feel. That fulfillment and satisfaction is amplified in looking back over our path, observing and owning our particular "roads not taken," and efforts to do more than generate profit and wealth. To be able to experience the reward of such heightened state of fullness while in this very lifetime is special, and could only have been achieved in a business entity that strives to be more than a financial enterprise. This is what I hope to pass on. The platform is in place and the foundational framework is embedded in our history, our culture, our commitment

We have agreed internally that Corporex as an entity is the platform for greatness. Indeed we believe that a corporation can be more than a financial enterprise—and if it can be, it should be!

Acknowledgments

I am grateful, sincerely grateful, to all the people we have worked with, not just inside the corporation but equally within the community, and especially to all the supporters, friends, family, executives, and partners—too many for sure to mention in the body of this publication.

There are so many people who have contributed to Corporex's success and to my own growth and development as an entrepreneur, community leader, man of faith, husband, and father, mentor, and there is no way for me to list them all here—the number of pages would rival the book itself. Some names you've already read within the book as part of pivotal events that happened in my life and corporate career. There are those and others who are equally important that I want to highlight, to acknowledge, and to thank for the pivotal role they played in helping me succeed, especially in those very early years in business. They also deserve my gratitude for their efforts in forming Corporex and supporting its transition into the springboard platform it can be, for the communities it will continue to serve.

Again, while I beg forgiveness for not mentioning all those who have been and currently are instrumental in Corporex's growth that I have not mentioned, you are no less appreciated for being a part of the journey with Sue and me and our family. There are more chapters to be written. But some of those who were there in the early stages, those who were not employed but served, those who have given decades in personal service and also played key roles, seem to come to the forefront for this occasion. They were key to getting Corporex off the ground, through tough decisions and conditions mostly in the early years of our formation, and they were the ones who helped me with personal achievements and need to be included in this particular publication.

Board Members in the Early Years

Great people with successful careers and abundant years of experience have given selfishly to the firm during fledgling periods. The financial compensation was nominal. I appreciate them so much.

George Scheper—George was Corporex's very first board of directors member. We built the board around George. He was a role model of a man, a model to me, and for many in and around the community. A caring father to nine children. He was witness to the power imbedded in strong values, high character, and the potential to reach the highest ranks of corporate stature and success, despite not having graduated from high school. He served effectively as chief financial officer and then president of DuBois Chemicals, and then as executive vice president of Chemed Corporation. Wherever he was, his presence was felt, including on our board, and you knew it was for the right reasons. Before the term "lead director" was coined, he served in that role for our company.

Edward Kulik—At the time that he joined the Corporex board, Ed was senior vice president of Massachusetts Mutual Life Insurance (MassMutual) and the company's top global real estate officer. It was Ed who suggested that Corporex locate its first branch office in Tampa, Florida, because he saw it as the next high-growth city, which had little competition at the time. We were so fortunate, blessed, really, to have a man of such stature on the board of directors of such a small entrepreneurial enterprise in its early years.

John Klare—John joined Corporex from the savings and loan industry in 1970, when the company's annual revenues were only $1 million. He put in place our first internal accounting systems, became quickly entrenched in every aspect of the business, and together we grew revenues five times in just four years. After the OPEC recession, John acquired a leading-edge robotic company in which we invested, but he remained on the board for more than 15 years thereafter. John was one of my closest friends and cohorts even before he joined the company, later became my brother-in-law and, until recently, was the only family member ever employed within the company.

Jerome S. Teller—Partner in the law firm of Katz, Teller, Brant & Hild (now Katz Teller), Jerry became one of my very best friends. We officially bonded when one time after lunch he wrote me a note: "I realized on the way home that in terms of our friendship, we have crossed a line of no return." I called him Sage, and he was recognized widely as a dean in the legal profession. Whenever I had a problem which was too complex, often involving personal feelings about business situations, I would call for a meeting with Jerry to help me sort it out. He would listen carefully and then provide a brilliant-but-simple solution. He served on the board of directors for nearly 20 years. The inscription on the glass doors of the Corporex Board Room identifies it as "The Jerome S. Teller Board Room," dedicated in commemoration of this skilled leader. No man ever had a better or more valuable friend than he.

Thomas Costello—Many, if not most, of my long-term personal relationships developed from business transactions with tenants. The best thing about the headquarters lease with Xpedx is the personal and professional relationship that evolved with Tom Costello, its CEO. Tom joined the board of Corporex and served for more than 25 years. He is a brilliant individual with incredible leadership skills who drove Xpedx from $600 million to $6 billion in revenues in just 10 years. He brought the same business prowess to Corporex's board meetings and to me at every opportunity. He and his wife Peggy became dear friends to Sue and me.

Paul Chellgren—When Ashland Oil relocated its headquarters to the Towers of Rivercenter, another long-term relationship developed. More than 30 years ago, as chairman and CEO of Ashland, Paul became a board member of Corporex. He is an accomplished, dedicated executive who has not missed one meeting in all of those years, and has been an astute advisor both to Corporex and to me. Paul's tremendous commitment of time and talent has been incredibly generous and selfless, and his counsel has been instrumental in Corporex's success.

Earlier Years Employees without Which We Would Not Be in Existence

I am forever grateful to Corporex's earliest employees, when the company was primarily a construction enterprise. Their efforts contributed to our success, then and now. Without them, there would be no book worth reading. Many people stand out in my mind and deserve recognition, but two contributors in particular were essential. Although they never expected or wanted recognition, Corporex would never have gotten to where it has without their hard work in the early days.

Howard Neltner—Howard was Corporex's very first construction superintendent and served the company for more than 25 years. He was loyal, hard-working, diligent, reliable, and crucial in those early years as we built the design and construction operations. It is difficult to properly describe his importance and the impact his efforts had on the success of the company, because he always gave his best, in good years and bad. He had a team of superintendents reporting to him, including Ted Finneseth and Jerry Kroger, and others for whom I will be forever grateful.

Ivan Wells—We called Ivan "Stonewall" because that is what first impressions of him suggested. He was a senior project manager who was responsible for many of our very largest projects for many years until his retirement. When we opened the Tampa office, Ivan, to my surprise, asked to be transferred there to start the construction operations. Under his leadership we built many buildings in Tampa, Orlando, and even the Goodyear blimp hangar in Pompano. For many years I stated that Ivan made more money for us than any other single person. He had a knack for purchasing frugally and delivering the savings to the company on those projects he supervised. He could walk onto a jobsite and instantly spot the smallest of problems. He was a man of extremely high virtue, integrity, and discipline that resulted in major financial contributions to the bottom line. He was the kind of man one could trust without limit.

Administrative Supporters

I have been blessed over the years with some of the most amazing supporters who worked side by side with me, helping to organize both me and my office. I cannot adequately express my appreciation for these ladies for all that they have done for me and meant to me and Sue over the years.

Sister Barbara Rohe—Sister Barbara was just Barbara Rohe when I hired her as my first secretary. Her administrative skills were incredible. Not only did she support my work, but simultaneously she kept 16 officers' and project managers' workloads functioning efficiently. I was always astounded to see her desk clean at the end of every day. She was truly a marvel. Because of that skill, we were stunned when she announced her decision to enter the Congregation of Divine Providence. She is now the Provincial of the Order over the entire United States. I knew she would rise above. Barb remained a part of Corporex in a spiritual way; her prayers and those of her sister nuns which she garnered for us over the years have no doubt helped us over many hurdles. I know that God sent her in the very beginning. We remain close to this day.

Wanda Ward—Wanda was so much more than a switchboard operator for more than 35 years; she was the face of the company. She had an incredible ability to recognize people, their voices, and to engage them whenever they called. Often that meant comforting them in difficult times and difficult situations; disarming was one of her most valuable skills. She is a person of deep faith. She was and is in our corporate DNA, she is imbedded in our heart. Her loyalty and her love are overwhelming, and we were blessed to have Wanda on our team and in our midst especially in the most difficult early years of our corporate career. She helped us get through those times, and I will forever be indebted to her.

Elva Malott—Elva dedicated 24 years to Corporex. For more than 20 years she was my right-hand assistant. A native of Northern Kentucky, Elva was an incredibly productive and trustworthy confidant who managed my office administratively. Elva is a special person who made me productive, made my life better, and she was with me through thick and thin, ups and downs, without end—a true supporter and work partner. She voluntarily testified to the grand jury on the Kenton County bidding scandal; I am pretty sure she laid down the facts with force, and that made a difference. Elva is a model for all to know and appreciate. In difficult years, we were able to overcome what seemed like unsurmountable challenges in large measure due to her encouragement and fortitude.

Therese Bottonari Lusby—Therese is another special person whom I was blessed to have as my assistant following Elva Malott's retirement. She fills the room with cheer and encouragement. I could count on her to lift everyone's spirits, even as we grappled with tough decisions. Her genuine caring and goodness were matched by her impressive efficiency and effectiveness at managing all of the work I piled on her desk daily. She also retired after serving Corporex for 22 years.

Executive Managers of Extraordinary Tenure

To adequately describe an entrepreneur's gratefulness for the special people who commit steadfastly and with loyalty for most, if not all, of their careers is not possible. They made Corporex possible, by working with me, night and day, to find opportunities and solutions to our challenges. Those employees who do manifest such durability and commitment are rare, especially in these times. These people made all the difference in my life and in the building of Corporex.

Thomas Banta—Tom has had one employer his entire career to date since graduating from Indiana University 38 years ago, and that is with Corporex. He has grown professionally over those years and tackled assignments well above his experience level from time to time. He has worked as employee and partner, too, served on boards, and been involved deeply in the community. He voluntarily testified in the adversarial Kenton County bidding grand jury probe, a process involving significant risk for him. To do so is akin to laying down your life for a friend, a boss in this case, and to speak the truth at whatever cost. Tom has been instrumental in much of the growth and decisions at Corporex. I am especially appreciative of his concern, care, and commitment to me and to all the people of the Corporex family of companies.

Dan Fay—I already mentioned Dan earlier in the book, but not in the context of longevity. Dan has been both an employee and a partner in the Commonwealth Hotels management enterprise. Our relationship began with our very first hotel project in 1984 and has prevailed now for 38 years. Dan has been a great partner and contributor to the success of Corporex as well.

Mike O'Donnell Jr.—Mike arrived at the young age of 28 as a graduate of the Ohio College of Applied Science in construction management, and at that very young age took total responsibility for the Lookout Corporate Center multistory office building, where our headquarters domiciled for nine years. He then built the 18-story Towers of Rivercenter. Mike did all the big jobs, especially the multistory buildings and complex developments, with very little help. He was in the office at 6 a.m. every day, including Saturday for a half day, consistently for 37 years until he retired. One cannot mention Mike without including **Mike O'Donnell Sr.,** who also worked for the company, reporting to his own son, for almost as many years. Together they were an impressive team. Corporex has been clearly blessed with the outstanding commitment to service and steadfast loyalty from the O'Donnell family, and we are forever grateful.

Jeanne Schroer—Occasionally a special person comes into your life. I have been blessed with many special relationships and bonds in the course of my career and none are more valuable than with this highly skilled, dedicated, and sensitive executive who came to us in her 20s. Equipped with four degrees in real estate and finance, Jeanne underwrote and constructed the story on our projects in a highly professional, easy-to-understand form. In the 1980s, she and I travelled the U.S. making presentations to bankers for loans on speculative office and industrial buildings. And we were successful in large part due to her. Her most pivotal accomplishment was to gain the commitment of two of Canada's largest banks to partner on the Rivercenter office building and hotel. Despite being initially turned down by 44 banks, she did not give up and made that project possible. She made huge contributions to the success of Corporex and remains today a strong partner in our community's advancement as CEO of the Catalytic Development Fund Corporation.

Mark Arstingstall—"I want to find a way back to Corporex" was his opening line when we met in 2001 over breakfast. He had worked here for nearly 10 years when he left to be president of am office-distribution enterprise. He returned after 11 years and worked nearly 20 more as chief accounting officer and controller, until retirement. Today he continues to serve on the family trust advisory board and as a key investment committee member on market securities. Mark has been an extremely loyal and committed, steadfast, and reliable officer whom I deeply appreciate.

Eagles in My Life

I call the following folks eagles because they hold a high position in my mind, have supported and served at the highest levels of bondedness and partnership, both to me personally and to the company. They have big wings, are a source of strength, are always there in multiple capacities, not necessarily directly for Corporex, but always for me—and I for them.

Robert Sathe—Bob is and always will be a part of my daily life. Wherever Bob is, he brings goodwill, he brings energy. He led the Connecticut General office when, in 1982, he took a leap of faith to locate the company's operations in our Lookout Corporate Center building. Since that move he has been a tenant ever since, for 40 years as both his businesses and Corporex grew and advanced . . . . Bob has been a full partner in moving the community forward, helping the less hopeful, and also in caring for Sue and me, too. We have been blessed to know and share deeply with Bob and his wife, Dell Ann. He has been a board member of Corporex for nearly 30 years and is also a member of the advisory committee to the Butler Family Trust and multiple other community organization boards where we serve together in shared community spirit. He has been a true friend, advisor, and partner.

Martin C. Butler—Marty is known and held dear by all. He is likely the most sophisticated real estate legal mind in the entire Greater Cincinnati area. For complex projects he is the go-to guy by bankers and, of course, by Corporex. After many years of providing legal services to all of our companies, we were so fortunate to have Marty join the board of directors of the company. I am proud and grateful for him, deeply appreciative of his service, his commitment to our company, and to me personally over his entire career in law, and, well, his life. It would be impossible to measure the magnitude of his contribution to the growth and success of our company, and I have benefited greatly from his friendship at the same time. We are aligned in spirit of service and the obligation we feel to help the less hopeful. Marty is the chairperson for the Butler Foundation, also of Urban Community Developers, and also on the advisory board of the family trust. Being nine years younger, he will carry the missions forward. I am blessed to have Marty as my sibling.

D. James Shea—Jim is my college buddy. We studied engineering side by side. He is a wise individual with a big heart and a keen sense of loyalty—humor, too. He is one who can be consulted on personal matters and hold them confidential. He is thoughtful and kind. They say a man's best friend is his dog—not so, not in this case. I could never have imagined a better bond than that which he and I enjoy. He is the best and longest-term friend I have had outside of work and family relationships, and he has been a blessing in my life and that of my entire family. I have gained from our relationship in ways that surely have helped Corporex to grow and to be successful.

Wayne Carlisle—I call Wayne my foxhole buddy because he is the kind of guy you want next to you in threatening times. Our relationship began when Corporex started doing business with his national crane rental company more than 40 years ago. He has a unique sense of people which he has generously shared with me, and from which I learn. We have partnered frequently on local projects, given financially too, with an eye to advancing the community in which we both were born, especially the urban river cities that both he and I call home. Our collaboration on key projects that will shape the future of our One NKY community will yield benefits for generations.

Jack Williams—I always said that I learned immensely from my relationship with Jack. We played tennis singles two to three times per week for 18 years, until he injured his back. We were different guys in most ways in life and wants. He was down to earth, loved to read and discuss philosophy. Jack was a people person with many close friends, likely because he proactively nurtured them. Upon delivering his eulogy, I stated, "Jack only worked hard enough to play," and he taught me that there is more to life than work. He wanted balance, and I learned to relax and slowed a bit thanks to the example he set. He was a special guy who changed me for the better as a result of our friendship.

Norbert Baumann—Norbert and I met at a Cursillo weekend 55 years ago and have been spiritual partners ever since. He was a market research guru for Procter & Gamble and traveled the world to gain knowledge about what P&G needed to develop to be ready for what the people would want 20 years into the future. His thirst for deeper knowledge of God, the universe, and truth were never ending. We shared deeply and often with each other in the early years about our respective findings and conclusions. He has been a strong influence and contributor to my own resolution and beliefs, and a helper to frame our deeper mission at Corporex.

Special Appreciation

To Dr. Marcia Layton Turner, author, and my writer and coach in the penning of this book. We agreed up front that we would strive to be partners in the journey that encompassed nearly 18 months. She has been gracious with her support and willingness to let me express fully what was in me to say. I am truly grateful to her, a peach of a person, smart, patient, and professional.

About the Author

William P. "Bill" Butler was born in Covington, Kentucky into a family of nine children. He was educated in the Catholic parochial schools and a Jesuit high school and secured an associate's degree in civil/structural engineering. A self-made entrepreneur, he entered the commercial construction and development business at the age of 22 and built Corporex into a national powerhouse. Bill and the company are known for having a commitment to contribution as a way of life, which manifests in charitable gifts and service, as well as efforts to advance the community where Corporex is headquartered.

He has been married to Sue Lutz Butler for 55 years and has two children and four grandchildren.